View from the dock
Diary of a Court Interpreter

CORDELIA NOVAK

Copyright © 2019 Cordelia Novak & Nikki Adams

Publishing: Nikki Adams hello@eaazone.com

Design by Ernesto Mora: eamora2012@gmail.com

ISBN:9781676346371

All rights reserved.

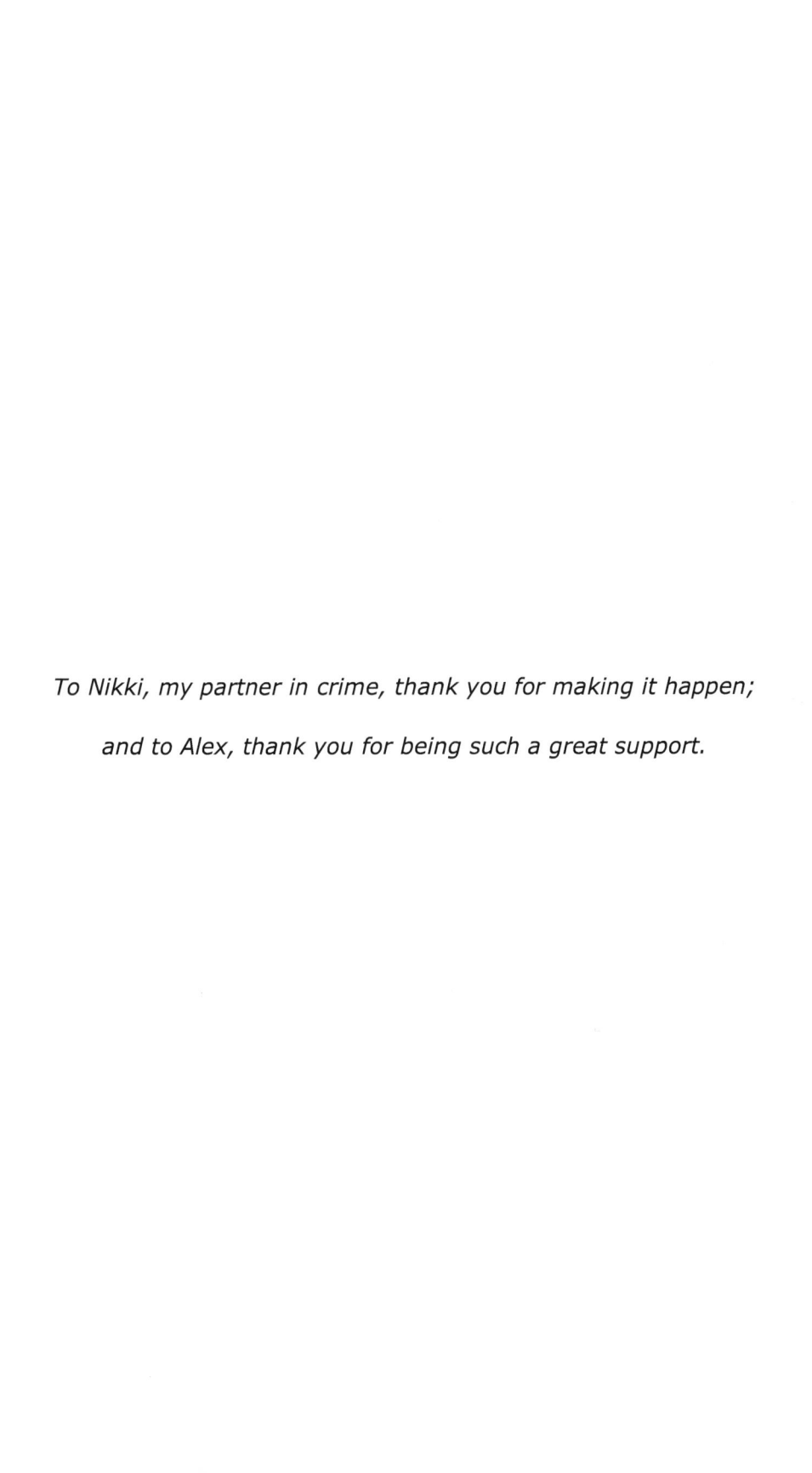

To Nikki, my partner in crime, thank you for making it happen;

and to Alex, thank you for being such a great support.

A Note from the Publisher

Having known Cordelia for many years, I have always been in awe of her daily encounters with British law enforcement which in turn allowed her to gain a unique perspective into otherwise not so unique situations. When Cordelia decided to write about her experiences and to share them with a wider audience, I was excited to get involved in publishing this sensational piece of writing.

View from the Dock offers exactly that, a back-row seat in a courtroom, next to the defendant and, in this case, their interpreter. Best seat in the house, save possibly, for the judge.
The dock is often separated from the rest of the room by a glass panel. This simple security measure can create a peculiar sense of detachment from the proceedings, which in turn allows the dock inhabitants to gain an unusual perspective on what unfolds directly in front of them. View from the Dock invites you to share this unique glimpse into nuances and vagaries experienced by those involved in the implementation of justice.

I'm truly honoured to have been part of this project.
I hope you will enjoy reading this as much as I did.

Nikki Adams

London, October 2019

CONTENTS

A Note from the Publisher	v
Prologue	ix
Court Interpreting - is it for me?	xii
Magistrates Court - Petty Crimes Big Dramas	1
Fun and Games at Magistrates' Court	1
Simple, Speedy, Summary	3
Rollercoaster Day	5
Bail Application	7
Twists and Turns in Suburbia	10
Better Person Than Me	12
Jogging for Justice	14
It Takes Two	17
Small Town Courts	19
Backwater Justice?	19
Justice-by-Sea	21
We Do Like to Be Beside the Seaside	22
When Love Goes Wrong	26
Making Sense of Domestic Violence	26
Love Conquers All	28
Communication Gap	30
Crown Court - When It Gets Really Serious	33

The Interpretation of Murder	33
Changing Lives, One Word at A Time	35
Floater	38
Courtroom Drama Nitty-Gritty	41
Trials and Tribulations	45
Gender Discrimination Within Criminal Justice System	50
A Week in The Life of a Trial	53
Knife Crime	57
My First Time	59
My Big Fat Trial	62
Justice Without Borders	69
Extradition of Damian	69
No Longer Welcome	74
High-handed Hague Justice	76
Forced Adoptions. When life punches hard	78
End of An Era	80
Stepping Out of the Dock	83
Interpreting in the Community	83
A Day in the Life of a Telephone Interpreter	88
Hi, I am your Polish Interpreter, how may I help you?	91
And Another Thing	95
Justice subject to Delays and Cancellations	95
Your Honour, My Lord, Your Worship	96

Defending the Guilty	99
Priceless Moments and Pet Frustrations	101
My Craft	110
Q&A – Do Judges Have Hammers?	114
Glossary	117

Prologue

At first glance my client Gustaw, might have been a victim of road rage himself, as a cyclist riding so slowly in a bus lane, as to enrage a young black driver behind him. They traded insults and engaged in a hit and miss spitting match.

Gustaw is now on trial for racially aggravated common assault as he allegedly called the black guy, a stupid black fucker during the shouting match, in response to being called a white cunt.

A bizarre bike versus car chase ensued, only for the incident to return to where it started a few minutes later. During the second round Gustaw smashed the car window to stop the driver from driving away before the police arrived.

Gustaw previously pleaded guilty to common assault by spitting, and criminal damage for the car window. I needed the basic story retold three times before it began to make any sense, which is why it's jumbled up here, few court cases are straight forward.

The only issue for the crown court jury to decide now is whether these offences were or were not racially motivated. Bearing in mind average cost of a crown court trial this has now become a £25,000 question....

The judge, the prosecution and defence counsels delve into this question to the depth and level of detail which makes me lose the will to live, and my client's eyes to glaze over. Case law is being pondered upon; Baroness Hale's name called in vain. '...needs to prove that either the entirety or a part of the defendant's hostility towards the victim was based upon his membership of the ethnic group...', '...was the use of the word black a demonstration of hostility, or is it indeed possible that only the word fucker was used as a demonstration of hostility and the word black, although no doubt having the capacity of being interpreted as emotionally charged racial epithet, used here as a purely gratuitous term, stating the obvious fact that the victim was indeed black...', I resurface every now and again from that sea of words and glance at Gustaw who has clearly given up any attempt to keep up with what I am whispering in his ear and is focusing his attention on picking dirt from under his fingernails instead.

During a short break Gustaw expresses his admiration for my interpreting skills and his gratitude for my willingness to apply these skills fully to his case.

In fact, he feels so pleased with the quality of my services that he decides to reward me with some valuable advice on the subject related to the theme of his trial.

He tells me that all black people carry baseball bats, knives and machetes in their cars, and advises me never to speak to any black men, especially young ones, especially in East London. I remind myself that he is on trial for using racially abusive language, the charge he categorically denies, whilst at the same time spitting at a young black man, the charge he pleaded guilty to at the previous hearing.

After the ceremonial court rise, followed by oyez oyez oyez and solemn head bowing, the judge and the prosecutor enter into a gloriously eloquent exchange, which, stripped of the decorum the location imposes on them, translates into this;

Judge: Why the fuck has this case been allowed to come up all the way to my court?
Prosecutor: Not an effing clue, mate.

The judge continues his rant, cherry picking his words from a more traditional court speak vocabulary.

He makes it known that in his opinion the court's precious time is being wasted on this absurdly narrow issue, and let's not lose sight of the fact that it looks like nothing more than a case of excessive road rage and both parties are equally to blame and the issue who is the victim and who the baddie here was most likely decided on the strength of who reported it first to the police, and since my client would have required an interpreter during a 999 call, he was most likely put on hold whilst the police operator requested the interpreter, and the other guy got through first.

Every now and again the judge tries to involve the defence barrister in this preliminary discussion, by addressing him directly, but the barrister seems to be a couple of steps behind the other two and he just says weakly, I am in full agreement with your honour, which only adds to the judge's frustration as it is clear that on top of being lumbered with an absurdly trivial case, he is being denied a chance of a good legal banter because one of the players is not up to it, or perhaps could not be asked.

My client's powers of intellect preclude him from understanding anything of what is currently being said no matter how well I interpret it. I say this with complete confidence, as I had spent the whole morning being subjected to his verbal incontinence while we were waiting for the courtroom to become available. I did my best to switch off, but I did not manage to block him off entirely, and so for example, I was told that the latest hurricane in the Caribbean was, obviously, a man-made machine-operated phenomenon, designed to reduce the overcrowding of our planet. Unfortunately, I think unkindly, he was not in its path.

At the end of giving live evidence to the court, my client adds his personal touch to the previous discussion among lawyers about what constitutes racially motivated hostility. When asked by the judge whether he would be offended to be called a white cunt, Gustaw looks puzzled for a moment. "Why would I be offended, your honour? I am white, so I don't mind if someone calls me white. And if someone wants to call me a cunt, that's their problem".

He pauses, looks around and decides to take full advantage of his moment in the limelight so he adds, "I have lived in this country long enough to know that black people sometimes take offence at being called black, and I recognise that being called a black fucker would be offensive to a black person, and so I would never call anybody a black fucker, because then the f....., he might beat me up."

He goes for his grand finale.

"Myself, I don't mind being called white anything because - ", he shrugs, outstretches his hands, and looking straight at the jury, finishes off, with unmistaken superiority in his voice "- because I am white".

Thank you, no further questions for this witness, your honour.

This is why I love my job, and why I put up with long commuting times, low pay, and lack of appreciation or interpreter rooms at courts. In moments like this this all is forgiven.

It took the jury less than an hour to reach a unanimous verdict that Gustaw's assault on his victim was indeed racially aggravated.

Court Interpreting - Is It for Me?

Let me introduce myself. My name does not seem to be of interest to anybody I meet professionally, I go by Madam Interpreter wherever I go, and I do go to a lot of places. For the last ten years my work took me to more Magistrates' Courts, Crown Courts, police stations, employment tribunals, probation offices, DSS tribunals and mental health facilities than I thought existed in the country, over eighty-five different venues on last count. I work mainly in and around London and the South East of England, and only occasionally further afield. I love my job.

At the same time, I acknowledge that fascinating as it is for me, legal interpreting might not be the right choice for everyone. In fact, you should only consider becoming a court and police interpreter if you love the idea of court and police interpreting. Do not do it if you like being appreciated, or well paid for that matter. In fact, if the latter is the case, make sure you stay as far away from legal interpreting as possible. Become an Eastern European lorry driver and smuggle cocaine in your spare tires instead.

Some personality traits are generally considered useful in this job. You should enjoy talking to people. It helps if you do not break into cold sweat at the very idea of speaking in public. It might thwart your efforts to appear confident when translating live evidence to the jury if you do not like hearing your own voice in an otherwise silent room where everybody's eyes are on you if only to hook their visual focus on something. You are not the main center of attention, that role stays with the defendant throughout, but you are the only voice that the judge, the barristers and the jury understand and rely on when listening to a non-English speaking witness's evidence, so make sure you are ok with that.

Not being emotionally squeamish is another desirable characteristic. As a court and police interpreter you will find yourself in the middle of awfully upsetting, unpleasant, distressing, disturbing, desperate situations. A lot. Emotional maturity and resilience in dealing with such scenarios is a must. Practice makes perfect, and apparently, after the first ten thousand hours, everybody becomes an expert in whatever they do. After ten thousand hours of court interpreting you will become word perfect, and you will be accurately completing the whispered interpretation before the client finishes their original sentences, but if you are somebody who finds it impossible to watch child abuse awareness ads, or a puppy being left out in the rain, you might struggle to get through the first ten thousand hours.

I have also found over the years that having an open, forgiving and accepting mind is of assistance. It helps if you are one of these people who always want to see good in the world first and who hang on to this belief unless proved wrong beyond any traces of doubt. This is not essential but it smooths communication if you do not decide that your client is guilty as charged within minutes of meeting them. The phrase, "beyond reasonable doubt", is not used in court terminology in the UK any more by the way. Instead, judges' direct jurors to decide their verdicts on whether they are sure of the defendant's guilt, nothing else than sure will do.

No particular political affiliations are considered as either an advantage or a hindrance to court interpreting, although staunch anti-immigration extremists might find their views counter-intuitive to this career choice.

Finally, do not go into court interpreting if you crave a clear career progression path. The thing is that the moment you become a fully-fledged court interpreter, there are no further ladders to climb. Once you find yourself locked in the dock of Court Number One at the Old Bailey, squeezed between a murder suspect and a Category One security guard, and you are facing a judge draped in a purple robe, it is as good as it gets, you are at the peak of your profession.

Another word of warning. Public service interpreters are all freelancers and as such we are not exempt from the usual slings and arrows of freelancing world. Our work might not come to a complete halt, but rapid gear shifts can nevertheless be quite dramatic.

One moment you are seated in a grand oak-paneled court room listening to flights of oratory excellence by the most Dickensian of lawyers still gracing this land, mesmerized by their measured cadences, and the next day you are perched on a grey plastic chair at a community service induction session at your local Probation office, listening to details of how many unauthorized absences will generate a warning letter, or, and this is dropping the gear all the way down, you are at home doing telephone interpreting, helping an energy supplier customer to up a new account. I see saying "our daily standing charge is seventeen point zero seven two pence per day, and our electricity unit rate is sixteen point forty-three pence per kilowatt-hour", several times a day, as our industry equivalent to out-of-work actors serving extra shot soy milk caramel lattes to suited and booted customers.

Route to Court

A few very brief introductory words on the UK legal interpreting industry, and interpreting in general for that matter. Interpreting as a profession is not regulated in the UK, which means, we the interpreters, do not have a single body that governs or regulates our conduct. A few organizations aspire to such a role, but they have no formal powers over individual interpreters. Having said that, there are some widely recognized rules that interpreters and interpreting agencies follow. One of these rules is a self-imposed quality control put in place in order to maintain standards, I guess it can be called self-regulation. According to this rule in order to become a court interpreter, an interpreter is required to pass one of two industry-recognized exams, either a Diploma in Public Service Interpreting (DPSI) Law option or Diploma in Public Interpreting (DPI) previously known as Metropolitan Police Test (Met Test). Both qualifications are awarded by the Chartered Institute of Linguists.

The exams are hard, but unevenly so, year on year. Some texts in the last few years have been so challenging that, in my view, they were chosen by academically inclined examiners as much for their own intellectual enjoyment while assessing candidates' efforts as any other reason. It depends on your starting point but as a rough guidance these exams require several months of intensive preparation, and please do not believe anyone who tells you they are a walk in the park. They would only seem easy if you sat them after you have been a practicing court interpreter for a couple of years, but since you cannot practice without passing an exam first this is purely academic. Both exams test consecutive and simultaneous interpreting skills, sight translation and written translation prowess.

They are probably much more difficult pieces of translation and interpreting work than you are likely to ever encounter in your job. They set strict time constraints and other restrictive conditions that put candidates under a massive amount of pressure which does not remotely correspond to any real-life situation. Exam organizers might work with an assumption that if you emerge successful from this ordeal, you will be ready for anything a courtroom or police custody throws at you, linguistically at least.

Historically, courts used to book interpreters directly using a publicly available register of suitably qualified interpreters. That changed in 2011, and now court interpreting government contract is awarded to an interpreting agency of good standing. The contract is usually granted for five years, and after that time bidding starts again. Interestingly, last time this happened the agency holding the contract previously did not re-apply to have it extended for another five years. As a court interpreter you will be working for the government appointed agency as a freelancer, and depending on your language and geographical location, you will either feel like a top celebrity whose phone never stops ringing, or a beggar scouring the agency online portal hourly for scraps of work. Usual market forces of supply and demand apply. My working language is Polish, which means demand is high, Polish being, according to the 2011 census data, the second most commonly spoken language in England, but the flip side of the same statistics is that supply is high too, which occasionally results in five Polish interpreters chasing one petty criminal along the corridors of Croydon Magistrates Court until one of us corners him.

Whilst in court you inevitably meet solicitors and barristers on a daily basis, and if they like your style this opens up additional revenue stream of working directly for their law firms during conferences with clients either at their offices or during field trips, also known as prison visits. Most court interpreters dabble in a bit of private work for solicitors now and then.

Occasionally, we also do other type of interpreting work which comes our way as a result of our names being available to the public via National Register of Public Service Interpreters (NRPSI). NRPSI is an organization interpreter loves to hate, but we still, mostly, pay the annual fee and get a new badge, because well, that's a good question and I ask it myself every year, but do it anyway. I suppose we pay for my continuing presence on the register as an expensive status symbol. NRPSI accepts only fully qualified interpreters as members and they recognize only DPSI or DPI holders as being fully qualified, which means they see themselves as this elite interpreting club where only the best are good enough. Some agencies also require their interpreters to be NRPSI registered. NRPSI used to be a powerful body back in the day when courts and police contacted interpreters on the register directly. These days are long gone and now one agency holds all the court jobs in their hands. You will be lucky if you get a couple of NRPSI-generated jobs a year, and they are more likely than not going to be working with insurance company assessors hunting crash-for-cash scammers than high end assignments.

In the next chapters I am going to take you on a trip around Her Majesty's criminal and family courts, immigration tribunals, prisons and police cells. The journey will be as gripping as TV courtroom drama or your money back. Well, not literally, obviously, it's just a figure of speech.

Magistrates Court - Petty Crimes Big Dramas

Fun and Games at Magistrates' Court

It's best to start dispersing myths and urban legends straight away. People I meet are often under the impression that court life and what follows my job as a court interpreter is filled with nothing but fascinating cases, and flights of oratory brilliance reminiscent of TV courtroom dramas. Today I wish to start restoring a sense of reality. Today, I give you a morning at one of my local Magistrates' Courts, followed by an afternoon at another.

First victory of the day. My case is actually listed at the court I arrive at and not at a neighbouring court which sometimes happens and which means another 50 minutes journey on another bus.

I look around and try to locate my client. He is here all right, top to toe in a track suit, bright blue with white stripes, downy baby hair popping through shaven head, fully made up disco-ready girlfriend in tow. I come up and say to him chirpily, *dzień dobry, Mr Xski?*

He looks around nervously, gives me a suspicious look and says, in Polish, "Who's asking?" "Hi, my name is **Cordelia**, I will be your interpreter today". His body language change is Transformers-worthy. "Oh, oh, hello, oh so good that you are here, phew, I don't need to stress any more. But how did you know it was me?"

Let's call it professional instinct. I usually recognize my clients with ease, but of course I cannot be totally sure. So, I dare myself and if I accept the dare, I speak to them in Polish straight away. If it works, and it mostly does, I am seen as somebody invested with magical superpowers. When it doesn't work, I say sorry, scrunch my face awkwardly and sit down quietly. Of course, the proper, professional way of doing it would be to ask loudly, in English, 'Is Mr Xski here?' I have seen lawyers and other interpreters do it, but where is the fun in that.

We wait. I ask my client if he has a lawyer. He hasn't. Does he wish to speak to duty solicitor? He doesn't. Is today the first hearing in the case or has he been to court before on this matter? He thinks it's the last. Last week he was here but there was no interpreter so it didn't go ahead. They asked him if he pleaded guilty or not guilty to the charge of assaulting a policeman at the custody suite of a police station. He replied that he couldn't remember and didn't speak English. Case was adjourned until today. He tells me has a twelve months' suspended sentence hanging over his head, but it doesn't seem to bother him, he says it more as a way of making small talk. We wait.

List caller comes out, Mr Xski, please fill in the means form for the court. I have no means. Please fill it in anyway. We fill in the means form. Mr Xski is 23 years old. He has no income. It turns out his girlfriend with a sweet smile and supermodel looks is the breadwinner in their little family. He stays at home and looks after their 6 months old baby. My facial expression is world class poker but he feels the need to explain. 'You surprised? Why, she can earn more money than me, just look at her and look at me. And she speaks English'. I say nothing.

We wait. Shortly after 11am some punters get impatient. At the sound of raised voices, security guards begin to hover. Noisy customers misread the signs and try to befriend the guards. Calm restored for now.

List caller comes out again, collects Mr Xski's means form. Duty solicitor wants to speak to Mr Xski even if he doesn't want to speak to him. During conference Mr Xski becomes quite lively and re-enacts his drunken antics at the police station with worrying passion. His knee swings by too close to my face for my liking. The solicitor advises him to plead guilty. Mr Xski grudgingly agrees but he sulks after that.

We wait.
We wait.
And we wait.

We are asked to sit at the back of the court, we listen to the previous case. I catch the tail end of a surreal assault story, involving a father, a set of twins, and a schizophrenic older brother. I switch off for a while. Mr Xski's case is called on.

- Do you plead guilty or not guilty?
- Ok.

The court clerk frowns.

- What does ok mean, Mr Xski?
- OK means ok. It means yes, it means I've wasted enough time here today, yes, whatever, give me the fine, I want to go home now.

I interpret in earnest.

Mr Xski is fined £332 in total. The list of his previous convictions doesn't seem to be available, so when asked he says he has no previous. We leave the courtroom.

If anybody has a view on whether I should have disclosed the information about Mr Xski's previous convictions to the court, by all means write down your reasons. Just make sure you do not send your answers to me, because I am already busy forgetting this case, as I try to work out how to get to my afternoon case 15 miles away in less than an hour.

Simple, Speedy, Summary

I arrive for my afternoon case at 13.45. According to my online job details I am here to assist Mr B., and the job type helpfully states CJSS. Other job types include preliminary hearing, plea, trial, or sentence. This gives us, interpreters, at least a vague idea what to expect on the day. CJSSS stands for Criminal Justice: Simple, Speedy, Summary, and gives me no clues. CJSSS was introduced some years ago as a guideline for Magistrates' Courts to deliver justice speedily and efficiently, cutting down the number of hearings in each case. Let's see how this optimistic proposition plays out in this case.

Court day typically runs from 10am until 1pm, and then work resumes at 2pm until 4.30pm. Anything after that is considered late sitting and is to be avoided if at all possible, by all interested parties.

My client is not here. I let myself be known to the usher and take out my book. Case Histories by Jeremy Hutchinson. Since my waiting time at court is publicly funded, I try to choose topical reading material if possible, it's only fair. Fortunately, justice is such a broad term, Robert Galbraith murder mysteries fit in perfectly too.

Back to Mr B. or rather the absence thereof. The court is busy, so I am left alone for a while. I get engrossed in my book, blocking out all peripheral noises, dramas and occasional tears. At 4pm the usher comes out, signs me off and tells me that a warrant is to be issued for Mr B.'s arrest for non-attendance.

Later that night I see a new job with Mr B.'s name on it, for the next day. I accept it and am assigned to it.

The next day is day two of Mr B.'s simple, speedy case. He was arrested in the town center yesterday afternoon and is now in the cells. Back to my book for a couple of hours. Custody duty solicitor materializes herself at some point and we go down to talk to him.

Mr B. looks worse for wear. Sort of covered in soot and dust all over. He has sores on his hands which seem infected. When he opens his mouth, his breath smells so badly I breathe through my mouth to stop myself from retching, my eyes water.

I have met Mr B. before, but he cannot remember me. He lives in a hostel. He is an on and off recovering alcoholic. In the last few months he had stayed mostly on track with an occasional slip. A few days ago, life became too much for him again, he got badly drunk and started spitting profusely at the Edward VII statue outside Tooting Broadway tube station whilst shouting *kurwa jego mać* with all his might. The literal translation is *his mother is a whore*, but it is unlikely that Mr B. was directing his insults specifically against Queen Victoria at this point.

After the spitting and the swearing had gone on for a while, a female member of public approached Mr B. and asked him if he could possibly stop doing what he was doing and go home. Mr B. took exception to being told off by a stranger and transferred his full attention to the female. He spat on her and screamed a mix of Polish and English obscenities at her, before walking away. Somebody called the police. Mr B. was found slumped on a nearby bench, got arrested and was kept in a police cell until he sobered up and then released on bail to his hostel address, with the court date set for yesterday afternoon. Yesterday he didn't turn up because he got muddled up. He had so many appointments with so many various people, who could remember them all. So here we are at court today. He has no recollection of the night I question whatsoever, but he is happy to take the police officer's and the complainant's word for it. He pleads guilty to drunken and disorderly behaviour and to a low-level assault on the female. He has 18 convictions of similar nature to his name, acquired during the last three years.

The idea is that sentences for petty offences start lenient, which leaves scope for making them more severe each time. So, to start with, back in the day, Mr B. got a police caution, no further action. Then came a couple of conditional discharges, followed by fines, higher fines, and then a few community orders, supervision orders, including failed attempts at making Mr B. engage with alcohol intervention programs. Today he is potentially facing his first custodial sentence. He is quite philosophical about that. First time for everything, right? As it turns out, he gets a 4 weeks prison sentence suspended for 18 months. Mr B. never managed to stay out of trouble for more than a couple of months before so it's only a matter of time when he gets caught again and this sentence is activated.

Mr B. is high maintenance petty criminal. Every few weeks he requires attention of roughly eight to ten members of British justice system albeit for a short period of time. They include an arresting officer, custody sergeant, duty solicitor, interpreter, prosecutor, court clerk, judge and probation officer.

In all probability sooner or later Mr B. will move on to committing burglaries, which will then become aggravated by an addition of a weapon, and after serving a lengthy prison sentence will eventually be deported back to Poland, but not before thousands of pounds have been spent on 'processing' him at numerous courts, probation offices, and finally Immigration detention centres across England.

I struggle to find a suitable moral to this story, so I will leave you with a sense of exasperation and mild hopelessness. A frustration shared and all that. I feel better already.

Rollercoaster Day

Some days I have no idea how things will work out for me and the defendant from one minute to the next. If I were prone to exaggeration, I would call them rollercoaster days. Here's one of them.

Whenever I arrive at court and find out that my case is listed in a youth court, I automatically say to myself, God help me, repeatedly, and I am not a religious person. Youth court seems to be my luck of the draw today, so I go down to the basement, funny that, youth court rooms are often tucked away underground, I suppose just in case "yoof" attitude lives up to its reputation, which it often does, and this can be more than a little intimidating to other court users, and that's why I am trying to rope God in today. Youth court interpreting booking usually means that I will be interpreting for the youths' mother. The youth themselves usually speak good English, and does not require interpreters. They are also usually annoyed that an interpreter was booked for the mother at all, they would much rather keep mother comfortably in the dark about finer details of what is being said about them in court.

A few minutes later an officer in the case comes in and as we chat, she says that the defendant is actually not that young, so she is not sure why he is listed in the youth court, and then, after quickly assessing my own possible age, she adds hastily, at least not youth court young, he is in his mid-forties.

A few minutes later it turns out the case was listed in the youth court by mistake, and we evacuate to the ground floor. Thank you, God, for your fast-track intervention, I appreciate it.

The police officer also tells me that the defendant literally does not speak a word of English. It takes me a couple of minutes to adjust to the new scenario, so not a youth court, but a client close to my own age, and no English. I like the no English clients best. They provide me with the most rewarding working conditions, I need to translate every single word both ways, from the moment the client arrives and I feel properly useful. I don't particularly enjoy interpreting for clients who have been in the country for ten years and therefore think they know English well enough not to need an interpreter. The solicitor sometimes indulges their belief and gives them a couple of minutes to prove their linguistic prowess, during which time they express themselves in English to the full extent of their ability, and we listen to their moving story, 'When I alcohol no good no work very bad my missus not happy you know not good very hard', upon hearing that the lawyer politely suggests that perhaps we could use the services of the interpreter after all. Clients grumpily agree, adding jovially to me in Polish, winking as they do, well, since they booked you, you might as well earn your money.

Today is shaping up well. A middle-aged man with no English, here for a trial, which is always a pleasure to work on, as opposed to, say, first appearance in a GBH (Grievous Bodily Harm) matter which is too serious to be dealt with in the Magistrates court, so the hearing only lasts five minutes, the case is committed to the crown court and bail is refused promptly.

On paper the trial looks interesting. Assault on daughter's ex-girlfriend. The next piece of information the officer in the case volunteers puts a damper on things, she says she would be surprised if he turns up at all today, as he did not turn up for his second interview, they had to issue a warrant. Non-attendance is always a possibility, and it is always most disappointing, especially when I have already sat through half an hour of eager anticipation.

He arrives, wife in tow, both smartly dressed and friendly. The wife excessively so, she does not waste any time, and she begins to tell me everything about the case, her daughter's relationship with the complainant's, her own relationship with her daughter, and the level of her husband's current earnings.

The defendant cracks his fingers in silence. He does not have a solicitor, so the court has appointed him a 'section 36 solicitor', in the interests of justice. The provision is defined by section 36 of Youth Justice and Criminal

Evidence Act, 1999. This is the usual practice during a trial, whenever a defendant, for whatever reasons, has not engaged the services of a lawyer, and so the court assigns them a solicitor purely for the purposes of cross-examining prosecution witnesses, as it would not be fair to allow the defendant himself to do so. The solicitor asks him a few questions about the incident to prepare a line of questioning for the purposes of cross-examination of the complainant. Just as we begin to get to the nitty-gritty of who did or did not do what and to whom, we are being called in.

The judge asks if we are trial-ready. Defence confirm we are ready, I am raring to go, and then the prosecutor stands up and spoils it all by informing us that the complainant is not here and is no longer interested or willing to give evidence in the matter, and so the prosecution offers no evidence in the case. The judge dismisses the case and the defendant is free to go. We come to a screeching halt, ride over. I don't mind, I never had the stomach for The Big Dipper.

Bail Application

Today I was booked for a bail application hearing at a nearby Magistrates' Court. The job took over five hours to complete, at the end of which time a bail application was not lodged. My day consisted in the main of trying to get any sense out of the defendant's girlfriend, who was talking a lot, on several different subjects at once, real skill, including appealing to the Hague about the way her boyfriend had been treated by police since his arrest, the UK was still in the EU, right, they had not left yet, yes, we are still in the EU, I know we are, but are they, sorry, who is they, the UK, England, they, are they? Yes, the UK is still in the EU, for another year or so at least, phew, so I can appeal to the Hague, I am already working on it. I let this one die down quietly.

She then channelled her efforts into trying to contact her boyfriend's cousins' wife to ask her to provide a bail address for him, initially focusing full attention on attempting to retrieve the boyfriend's cousin's wife's telephone number from an ancient black Nokia, the type preferred by big baddies in TV crime dramas, and half of my clients, the other half opting for flashy latest models, funny that.

The antique phone was about to die, and since she had no credit on it, naturally, the barrister dialled the number, and as soon as the boyfriend's cousin's wife answered he passed the phone to me to talk to her in Polish, but I was not entirely sure what I was supposed to ask her, so the barrister fed me each line of conversation, could Michal stay with you and give his address as his bail address to the court, but why, why here, he and his girlfriend moved out of here, they were now renting somewhere in something Lane or something, but ok, yes, he can stay if there is no other way, ok, thank you, could I pass your phone number to the court police liaison officer (PLO) to verify that he could stay at your address, well, ok, if you must. Will you be available on this number for the next few minutes, yeah, ok, and then she disconnected. The PLO called the number a few minutes later but the defendant's cousin's wife must have changed her mind, as the PLO looked confused and told us, no, not really, this address is not suitable, the lady is not happy for him to stay there for any longer than a week or so, because she sees him as troublemaker.

The girlfriend then wrote down another address, to give to the court as a possible bail address, we asked her whose address this was, she said it was temporarily her address, as she and her boyfriend's cousin's wife did not see eye to eye so she had recently moved out of their place. But I thought Michal said that you were living together, barrister interjected, yes, well, we are, we are together, and we used to live together and I am sure we will again, but for now this is where I live. Will the landlord of this place confirm that Michal could live there with you, oh, no, I am sure he would not agree to that, he specifically told me that I was only allowed to live there by myself, and anyway this is only a single room. So, we cannot really put forward this address as a bail address for Michal, can we? Yeah, no, you are right, you cannot, not really. We exchange desperate glances with the barrister.

We go into court, I sit down in the dock next to the defendant, the judge is not there, so we wait, the client asks me if Beata, that's the girlfriend, give me his cousin's address, I say, yes, she did. I tell him that that unfortunately this address is not going to work out, why not, because your cousin's wife was not happy to let you stay there for more than a week, he swears under his nose, punches the wooden bench next to him hard, puts his head in his hands and shakes it, he says he will kill himself if he doesn't get bail today, the guard asks me, interpreter, what is he saying, he seems distressed, I say, he says he is going to kill himself if he doesn't get bail today. This makes the guard jump up, he picks up the phone in the dock, whispers something, a couple minutes later two more guards appear, he talks to them on the side, I cannot hear them, after a while the first security guard asks me to tell him that if he is refused bail and goes back to prison he is going to be put on suicide watch, because of what he has just said, the defendant looks at me with disbelief and his desperation goes up a notch, which neither he or I thought was possible a couple of minutes ago.

The judge enters, we all get up, the judge acknowledges us with a nod, he sits down, and we sit down. The defendant has an idea, and he acts on it immediately, he says in English, please stop, please my friend, and then switches into Polish, and says to me, I need to speak to my barrister again, now, I have a great idea about the bail address, I need to speak to him now, before we start, I raise my hand to draw the court's attention to the dock, the defendant would like to speak to his barrister, your honour, the barrister approaches the dock, I whisper to him through the glass, he wants to speak to you before we proceed any further, we go down to the cell, the defendant says, I want Beata to use my wages, which should be in my bank account by now, and rent a room for the two of us, and then we make a bail application when she has done it, I do not wish to make one today. We go up to the court again, the defendant is taken back to prison, and his case is committed to the Crown Court, to be heard in 28 days. The barrister will make another bail application to the Crown Court when all parties are ready.

On the way to the bus stop I spot Beata's white puffer jacket in front of me, so I slow down my pace to put a safe distance between us. I have had my fill of misery for one day, I really do not feel like listening to it all over again, and this is no doubt what would happen if she caught my eye now.

Beata is walking slowly too, so I stop, take out my phone, and pretend to read a just-received message. Then a WhatsApp message does arrive, I read it, and respond to it. When I look up again, she is gone. I feel strangely drained by today's experience, even though the case was hardly challenging, professionally, and it was not even a particularly upsetting scenario. Perhaps it was just one sad story too many in quick succession. Whatever the reason, I wish to forget about it and move on with the rest of my afternoon. I sit at the bus shelter, I enjoy an unexpected moment of warm sunshine and savour the equally unexpected momentary contentment, the feeling that all is well and good with the world, my world at least. And then I see Beata's intense face right in front of me, as clearly as if she still was there. She isn't, she is long gone, running away, chasing something, who knows, but I realise I am stuck with her and her distress, not ready to get her out of my system just yet, and so her deeply unhappy expression lingers on in my mind.

Suddenly, a thought strikes me, I deal with a lot of profoundly unhappy people. This realisation is not exactly ground-breaking, bearing in mind I work with people accused of committing serious criminal offences, or being subject to family court proceedings, but still, it hits me today with epiphany level strength. I handle a lot of unhappiness on a daily basis. Something is always painfully missing from the lives of people I assist linguistically. Most of them are lonely, poor, unloved, suffer mental or physical ill health, have no job, no family, no home, or all of the above. They carry their unhappiness with them wherever they go, next to their tobacco and rolling papers.

I cast my mind back to hundreds of hours spent rubbing shoulders with my unhappy clients over the years. Has it changed me, have I learnt to appreciate my own life more, has it made me a more grateful, humbler, better person, or have I just managed to stay immune to their unhappiness and remain safely detached from their lives? Hard to say, I might be too close to see it, and I am not usually prone to navel gazing anyway, I just get on with my life without excessive self-analysis. If I thought a bit more about how I spend most of my days elbow deep in misery, I might find it depressing and alarming, I might start wondering why so many people have said to me, "I don't know how you can do your job". My knee jerk reaction is that somebody has to do it and since this is what I chose to do for a living, it makes sense to be me. I try not to analyse it beyond that, which is probably self-preservation kicking in.

Twists and Turns in Suburbia

I like to think that the very nature of my work protects me from falling into the rut and that my days can end up being many things but they are unlikely to be mundane and predictable.

This is true enough most of the time but every so often a call comes through in the morning and within minutes I am on my way to a suburban Magistrates' Court looking forward to nothing much except a last-minute urgency uplift to my regular hourly rate, my suburban sanity supplement.

On Magistrates Court days my job consists, in the main, of sitting around in waiting rooms, staring at rows of grey plastic chairs and floor tiles for hours. Waiting time can be anything between one and six hours per day, followed by a short frantic hour or so of actual interpreting. It was the abundance of just such waiting time that got me started writing this book. This meant that I could spend my court waiting time writing about my court waiting time rather than just doing the waiting. Much more productive than staring at floor tiles, and the time passes much quicker too.

Today the waiting room is overflowing. Folk who live in this area must be a strongly family orientated crowd, each defendant is surrounded by a small army of spouses, sprogs and siblings. That means loud gum chewing, stilettos, full make up, black lace mini dresses at 9.30 in the morning, buggies, McDonald's balloons, crying babies, toddler tantrums, the lot.

I report to a manic looking list caller who puts a tick against my client's name, already talking to the person behind me as she does that. The list caller is a person with a clipboard, whose job it is to match everybody on their daily list of cases with everybody in the waiting area.

No seats available so I prop myself against a windowsill and wait. I spend the next two hours avoiding grubby little fingers, balloons, paper airplanes, and especially any eye contact. Several people attempt to talk to me. They ask for time, clearly distrusting a clock prominently displayed on the wall; for a lighter, clearly failing to notice my perfect smoke-free complexion; they enquire whether I am a solicitor, clearly noticing my Mulberry handbag, a solicitor staple, and in my case a result of unexpectedly successful campaign appealing to my loving husband's Christmas generosity.

At 11.15 the list caller comes out and inspects the status quo. She is desperately trying to remember who is who and who to call on next. I give out no clues. Public service interpreters are on a very modest hourly rate, time really is money for us.

Midday arrives and I can almost hear the bottom of the barrel being scraped as court users desperately try to find something to keep themselves entertained. That barrel was never very full in the first place. They now pace up and down the length of the room, shake their heads robustly, chew on their lips, and generally give the impression of seriously tormented human beings. I, in the meantime, reach the end of second chapter of my book. Suburban Magistrates' courthouse employs a puzzlingly large number of security guards. They have gathered in a merry group in the corner to discuss last night's footie. They go over the match in such detail I look again to double check that they are not actually watching the game as they talk. Their impassioned commentary drowns out any other noises for a while. I try to block out their jovial outbursts to no avail. List caller comes out of Court One again. This time she comes up to me, *are you a Romanian interpreter, no, I am Polish, oh, ok, we haven't got any papers yet about your client, so I am afraid I am not sure when you will be able to go and see him.* Music to my ears, thank you. I do not actually say it aloud, or at least I hope I don't.

12.59. Court Number One is locked for lunch hour. The sanctity of the lunch hour is totally untouchable, sixty minutes, not a second less. I walk to a nearby town centre, visit the same shops as usual, M&S, TKMaxx, Pret, Café Nero, sit on a bench, eat my usual coronation chicken sandwich, drink regular cappuccino, chocolate on top. Back at the waiting room at a quarter to one. Several other faces from the morning session return, new ones appear. Can't be much longer now.

Another hour passes and then suddenly, 'Polish interpreter?' a solicitor holding a pile of papers is ready for me. We go down to the cells for a conference. My client is an overnight case on allegation of criminal damage to hospital equipment and being a nuisance to A&E staff while drunk. I am not sure if being a nuisance is a legitimate criminal offence, but there we go. The only thing still on his mind today is that earlier that day a smartly dressed gentleman gave him a ten-pound note. He had it in his backpack. Yes, he was drinking, because that is what he does, he is an alcoholic, he drinks. Then, an ambulance picked him up because, as usual, they felt they had to save him, he sounds bitter about that. Unfortunately, his backpack was left behind and so the crisp slinky new ten-pound note was now lost for ever. He does not seem bothered about the rest of his belongings, but it is not very often that a kind elegantly dressed man would give him money, and a whole £10 note too. The more we talk, the solicitor trying to obtain simple instructions, the more obsessed he sounds about the note. It transpires he had got into a rage when he realised his backpack did not make it to hospital with him, so he grabbed the first thing within reach and smashed it onto the floor. That thing happened to be a computer; hence we are where we are.

Later that day, after the district judge gives him conditional discharge and he goes on his way, the £10 note still not forgotten, I think to myself, what would it be in my case, what would it take to send me over the edge like that? I like to believe that would simply never happen, no matter what, but then again what do I know about being a homeless alcoholic in a country whose language I do not speak? Would it really come to one shiny banknote capable of buying me, what exactly? A bottle of cheap cider, some food? Would it not have to be the prospect of losing so-called everything, my family, my home? Then again, perhaps my client had lost all of that already, and the note had become his everything on that day.

Suburban Magistrates' no longer feels a pain in the neck. I feel humbled by the encounter with my client, and a profound existential sadness overwhelms me.

Better Person Than Me

Debriefing sessions for public service interpreters who work on particularly distressing legal, medical and social services assignments is a subject that comes back up every so often in industry discussions as a 'would be nice to have' support service, rather than a realistic prospect. Personally, I feel that years of experience made me confident to take on board even the most gruesome and disturbing events in my stride as they are being related to me, and just get on with it. All in a day's work. What I would benefit from however, is advice on how to get over meeting some truly abhorrent human beings, and how to erase their stupid smirks from memory.

Some of my clients do such vile messed up things that it takes a bigger person than me not to feel disgust for them whenever our paths cross in the implementation of justice. It takes all my professionalism and will power not to show that disgust openly in court. Today the task overwhelms me and I fail.

Marcin is a tall muscular man in his early thirties. Messy blond mop of hair, very Polish face, round and flat, I am pretty sure as a fellow Pole I am allowed to call it a potato face without causing offence.

His nonchalant demeanour tells me he sees himself as Adonis-level handsome. He beams me a chummy smile as soon as he sees me. I assisted him during previous stages of current proceedings, so he thinks we are mates. I recognise him, and as soon as I do, I also recognise the repulsion I felt for him before, but can't quite remember details of the case.

This happens to me a lot. If I work with somebody more than once during the lifespan of their case, they assume that I will remember everything about them as soon as I see them again. Usually, I don't. I see so many of them, their looks and their stories overlap to a large extent, circumstances form a similar pattern, and typically feature several cans of strong Polish beer, an empty bottle of vodka, wife texting her boss or a work colleague, husband's jealousy, pushing, shoving, shouting, screaming, attempts to snatch the phone from her, kitchen knife, breaking the garden door, smashing a bedroom window, small children watching, crying, terrified, bruises to the face, arms or legs, threats to kill her, the children and himself, breaking the phone, falling asleep drunk on the sofa, or leaving the house just before police arrive. By the time we meet for the second time, sometimes months later, I have no recollection of exact facts in that particular matter.

My facial expression could not be less inviting but it does not deter Marcin. I have just been handed a copy of his pre-sentence report (PSR) prepared by probation, to translate to him. As I begin to read it is all coming back to me and I move away from him, instinctively, imperceptibly. He interrupts me every now and again with comments, excuses, whatever. I wait, silently, eyes firmly on the piece of paper in front of me, until he finishes his interjection, and I carry on reading. What would it take for him to get the hint that I do not wish to engage in any chit-chat with him and that I find him revolting?

The probation report mentions continuing lack of insight, persistent tendency to minimise the impact of his behaviour on the victim, flippant attitude to his own offending. He proves this assessment accurate every time he opens his mouth.

The offence was domestic assault with strong aggravating features. Details were that he poured a can of beer over his girlfriend's head, slapped her in the face and then punched her repeatedly in the stomach. The girlfriend was pregnant at the time. He screamed, 'I want it to die', during the sustained attack. Neighbours heard the disturbance and called the police. She was taken to hospital, with extended bruising, scratches and cuts all over her body. He entered a basis of plea, which means he admitted some facts, but not others. He only accepted pouring the beer over her head, and claimed that all her injuries were self-inflicted, because she wanted to get rid of him and the baby in one evening. He also maintained that she exaggerated and faked the severity of the pain she was in when police arrived, she had always been a good actress. In any event he couldn't understand what all the fuss was about, the foetus survived after all. The prosecution did not accept his basis of plea, trial followed, and he was found guilty.

At today's sentencing hearing Marcin was not legally represented, so the judge asked him if he wished to address the court himself in relation to the offence or express any thoughts about what, in his view, might be an appropriate sentence. Marcin cocked his head slightly, cupped his chin in his hand, smiled philosophically, and said, 'I don't even know if it was mine'.

He was sentenced to 16 weeks suspended custodial sentence, 180 hours unpaid work and 15 days rehabilitation activity requirement on the subject of domestic violence, as well as ordered to pay £650 prosecution costs. Leaving the court, he was no longer philosophically inclined. His anger barely contained, he walked off without a goodbye. It was my turn to smirk.

Jogging for Justice

In my glamorous Court Interpreter career each day is different, each client is unique, and travelling opportunities are endless, as can be seen from the timetable below. It keeps me fit too. What not to like? There really is no such thing as a typical day for me, each day writes its own story as it unfolds. Here's one of them.

7.15 Leave home in South London by car, youngest child in tow

7.35 Arrive at my daughter's school in Clapham, drop her off at breakfast club, thank God and Council for breakfast clubs, and wave goodbye.

7.50 Park the car in Streatham Hill and take 133 to Brixton. It is such a blessing that parking is free around there, it makes things tick along nicely in the mornings.

8.15 Arrive at Brixton underground station, take Victoria line to Green Park, change for Jubilee

9.05 Arrive at Southwark tube station and rush to local Crown Court via Pret cappuccino and egg and salmon breakfast baguette

9.20 Leave local Crown Court because it turns out I was booked in error as the defendant was not required to attend today. I am signed off by a bored court office worker. I had met her several times before, so I greet her with a big smile. She does not return the smile and asks me formally, how can I help you, which is cue for me that we are going to play this game in which she has no idea what possible reason I might have to attend court today, and in which we see each other for the first time ever that morning. I really don't mind, I play along, hiding my amusement. She tells me that even though she has no idea why 'they' booked me in the first place, I will be paid for one hour plus traveling expenses. I nod and smile at her. I know full well there is no 'them', and she is the one who books interpreters for the court, so she must have booked me in the first place for no reason at all. I wonder if she knows that I know.

9.30 Call my agency on an off chance that there might be a last-minute booking available somewhere, preferably in London, for today, and bingo, a couple of minutes later I get an urgent Wimbledon Magistrates booking for this morning, can I possibly get there before 10.30? Sure, no problem at all.

9.45 Board Jubilee Line at Southwark

10.00 Change at Westminster for District line

10.15 Change at Earls Court to Wimbledon branch

10.25 Get a call from my agency asking if I would be willing to accept a second Wimbledon booking for the afternoon. I graciously accept.

10.30 At Parsons Green, I realise that I should have walked to Blackfriars Overground train station from the Crown Court and taken a direct train to Wimbledon, and not the tube. Oh, well.

10.45 Arrive at Wimbledon station and sprint to court

10.55 Arrive at court, sign in at reception, sign in with list caller, say hello to my clients, a married couple on fraud charges, sit down for the first time today, eat Pret baguette purchased outside Southwark tube station nearly two hours before

11.30 Conference with duty solicitor who seems to be amused by certain aspects of the case. He decides the husband and wife will need two separate firms to represent them due to obvious conflict of interest. He chooses to represent the wife and asks the husband to leave the room.

12.30 Conference ends, I am trying to get hold of bail duty solicitor to represent the husband, none available till after lunch

13.00 Court breaks up for lunch, I sprint to local Pret for staple chicken and avocado sandwich and another cappuccino.

13.30 Back to court for my afternoon matter, pre-sentence probation report. The morning husband and wife matter will have to wait, probation waits for no one. Client is very chatty and doesn't take a hint when I am typing away these very words.

14.00 Probation appointment begins, suddenly client is no longer chatty, not volunteering any information. Hard work all along.

14.40 Probation job completed, back to the husband and wife case from this morning.

15.15 Case called on for transfer to Crown Court due to the seriousness of the charges

15.40 I leave court and sprint to Wimbledon station to catch 15.58 to Streatham.

16.15 arrive at Streatham station and take 109 to Streatham Hill

16.30 arrive at younger daughter's school just as they come out of sewing club. I compose myself just in time to make it look like I have it all perfectly under control and I timed my arrival with precision.

17.15 Arrive home after a long slog in near stationary traffic.

17.16 Greeted on the doorstep by my offspring; 'Mummy, Mummy what's for dinner, did you pay for my choir trip, can I go to Melissa's for a sleepover on Friday, and I need your help with French and history homework'

By the time I arrived home, I'd clocked up 15,383 steps on my Fitbit. I criss-crossed London expertly and ran everywhere. I feel like a walking talking Transport for London journey planner. Tomorrow, hopefully, my devotion to Justice will require less exercise.

It Takes Two

Some jobs are unbelievably slow going, they feel like wading through a muddy field, but much less fun.

It was 12.45 at one of my local Magistrates Courts, and I could hardly stay awake. Adrian, my client for the day, was equally lethargic. My Polish-man-in-trouble-with-the-law detector spotted him sitting all by himself in the furthest corner of the waiting room. The usher asked me to find out how he was going to plead. Adrian didn't know what he was charged with, he said there had been a street fight, and he'd joined in, and then he ran, and then the police caught him, he didn't know why he ran, he knew it was a stupid thing to do, but here you go. Adrian remembered a big fight and a friend of his getting a nasty cut to his head. This description of events could mean a number of different charges, from drunken and disorderly behaviour through common assault to affray, so the usher and I were none the wiser. For completion's sake Adrian added that since he didn't know what he was accused of, he didn't know how to plead, because, said with an unexpectedly philosophical slant, to know how to answer, you first need to know the question. I translated all this to the usher, who realised he would not be able to tick any boxes next to Adrian's name on his notepad just yet.

We all stared at one another for a while, but that did not provide any answers. The usher concludes that Adrian needed a duty solicitor, which might take a while. We passed the time by completing his "means form". It took skill and patience to drag basic financial details out of him. He was most disinterested in the whole procedure. Duty solicitor arrived, and after he tried and failed to extract any meaningful information from Adrian, he went away to look for 'the papers'.

The papers hold the key to every court case. They form the basis on which a solicitor advises clients how to plead. The papers would soon tell us what the charge was and the facts of the case according to the prosecution. Without the papers we would not progress past our current conundrum.

Sometimes the whole day passes by waiting for the papers. After years in the business it is still not entirely clear to me why the papers can be so hard to get hold of.

We broke for lunch and when we returned an hour later, the solicitor was still trying to locate the papers. My client had by then slipped into near horizontal semi-slumber.

What the papers revealed, when they finally materialised, did little to perk up our uneventful day. The charge turned out to be 'using threatening words or behaviour', the CCTV material was pretty conclusive and the solicitor advised my client to plead guilty. Adrian was likely to get a fine, or possibly even a conditional discharge if he was lucky. He looked almost disappointed that the charge did not turn out to be anything more exciting than that. After ten minutes in the courtroom the case was over, Adrian was fined £300 payable within 28 days. When he said goodbye to me, he looked bored out of his mind.

It was not until I was on the train home that I got rather excessively annoyed with Adrian. I resented his blasé don't give a damn attitude. In my line of work, it takes two to make each day interesting. If a client behaves as if he couldn't care less, it rubs off on me eventually and it is de-motivating and soul destroying.

I give it my best every day but I often find my clients are less enthusiastic about working with me, or engaging their solicitor, the system, anything and anybody.

Small Town Courts

Backwater Justice?

It is refreshing to travel to a small-town court every now and again. The moment I step into the building I am usually offered a cup of coffee and am being fussed over all day long. It is touching to see how much excitement the arrival of a humble Polish interpreter can evoke in those off the beaten track places.

Once, the witness care representatives offered to make me a cheese sandwich so I didn't have to walk to the town centre in the rain. I nearly fainted.

Today I am in a lovely, wisteria-lined, cobble-stoned corner of the country. As I leave the station, I slow down to be more in tune with everybody else's pace. A passer-by says hello to me as I walk down a leafy road, I look behind me to make sure the greeting is meant for me, a complete stranger, but there is nobody else, so yes, hello to you too, the sun is shining, birdsong at full volume, what not to enjoy.

I am here for a trial. The defendant is a Polish builder, dressed up in an ill-fitting shiny suit for the occasion. The complainant is his ex-wife, also Polish. The only contested charge is harassment by stalking.

This type of cases naturally relies heavily on mobile phone evidence, which is vital in establishing whether or not the alleged stalker continuously called and texted the alleged victim. Mobile phones of both parties were seized by the police early on in the investigation. Early September trial date was set in June.

The phones are still held by the police, but, and this is the first 'come again?' moment in the story, the mobile phone data was never downloaded, text messages never looked at, printed out, or translated from the original Polish. Nobody checked the number of texts sent by the defendant during the relevant period, and whether the alleged victim was replying to the messages, as the defendant claims she did, or ignored them completely as she claims she did.

This is frustrating to say the least, as the magistrates have to decide the case purely on his word against hers, even though abundant mobile phone evidence is sitting in the investigating officer's desk literally round the corner from the court. It has been sitting there for some five months, since April this year.

During examination of both witnesses, the prosecution and the defence refer to the text messages at length and the lack of the actual messages' transcript becomes more and more embarrassing as the day progresses. Let's move on.

The ex-wife, the only prosecution witness gives evidence first. She has great confidence in her English language abilities, so she has not requested an interpreter. As we discover with every misunderstood question, every incomprehensible answer, her confidence is totally unfounded. Awkwardness sets in as we listen to the series of miscommunications between her and the increasingly desperate prosecutor. Ten minutes into this ordeal it becomes obvious to everybody that the quality of her evidence could be immensely improved by the assistance of an interpreter.

You might be excused for thinking that the glaringly obvious solution would be for somebody in the courtroom to suggest that since we already have a Polish interpreter in the room, assisting the defendant, perhaps we could use her services to assist the prosecution witness as well. Unfortunately, the issue is rather more complicated, as flagging it at this late stage would open a small Pandora box of questions; why hadn't the need for the interpreter for this witness been highlighted earlier on in the process, and also, given how bad her English is, how reliable her written statement given to the police in the initial stages of the investigation is, plus, a delicate matter of who should say something now, should it be the prosecutor himself, the legal adviser, the increasingly bemused magistrates? Nobody says anything and we plod on, the witness giving ambiguous answers in broken English. I look around, the elephant in the room reclines comfortably in the corner, undisturbed in his slumber.

Both lawyers are young and inexperienced. Young inexperienced lawyers need to earn their stripes somewhere. Today feels ever so slightly as if we are all participating in a sophisticated role-play to allow them to do so. I hope the defendant is too nervous to realise this, because for him today is rather important. The defence barrister is forever flicking through her copious files, peppered with post it notes. She, at least, comes across as friendly and enthusiastic, whilst the prosecutor adopts a distinctly passive aggressive approach to the proceedings. They keep interrupting each other and both jump to their feet every couple of minutes. The magistrates look like they would rather be elsewhere, anywhere but here.

After lunch the defendant gives evidence, assisted by me, which immediately makes his version of events easier to follow and more coherent than that of the complainant's. He understands each question at first attempt, and answers in full sentences, offering additional explanation when asked.

After that the defence barrister makes her final submissions. Following the disastrous evidence from his witness this morning, the prosecutor sulkily forgoes his right to address the court, so the trial feels oddly lopsided. The moment the defence lawyer sits down, the magistrates rise hastily to deliberate. As the time is now five fifteen in the afternoon, we are already firmly into court overtime territory. They come back within minutes and announce the only decision they could reasonably deliver, given the imperfections of the evidence. The defendant is acquitted, we are free to go.

Has justice been served in this beautiful corner of England today? Should the trial have been adjourned to obtain the mobile phone evidence and to arrange for an interpreter for the complainant? How many more times will I ask myself similar questions as I walk down a picturesque tree-lined winding country lane towards a London-bound train?

Justice-by-Sea

Travelled to a seaside court today, after working in London for a while. There is something inexplicably refreshing about travelling out of the metropolis to help administer justice in sleepy small towns. First, it's the station announcements, the very sound of Shoreham-by-Sea, Goring-by-Sea makes me put an invisible straw hat on. Next, come the seagulls. Their squeals, guaranteed to be the first sound I hear as I walk out of any seaside train station set the tone for the day. Finally, it's the local lads, Ill-fitting borrowed suits barely covering prison tattoos and spiky attitudes. Middle-aged mothers reverting back to babysitting mode, making sure their grown-up offspring make it inside the courtroom without straying at the last minute. The way they skilfully fill in their sons' and daughters' mean forms, for they could run tutorials for MPs completing expense forms. Frustrations simmer just under the surface; a few bubbles escape every so often. I cut an odd solitary figure amidst gum-chewing friends and family support groups. Minutes roll slowly away, in rhythm with rizla wrappers. Eleven o'clock. Patience is wearing thin for some clients. They all demand to be seen next. I am the only one keeping my cool. My client has not turned up. I am released until after lunch when I have another case. As I walk towards town centre, I am totally relaxed, and I smile to myself. Seagulls eye my sandwich beadily and it all feels like a mini-break. The familiarity of it all is therapeutic and I almost forget that I am at work here. It is definitely the case of regular dose of seaside courts keeps the doctor away.

We Do Like to Be Beside the Seaside

I must be one of very few nice people I know who has a vested interest in crime figures going up, and who acknowledges rising alcohol consumption levels among immigrant population with calm. Court interpreters languish in law-abiding times and places. Increased levels of national prosperity and contentment is not good news either. The more frustration and pent-up anger all around is better for job security. I should be in demand for years to come.

Perhaps somewhat counterintuitively, then, humour plays a big part in my job. Spending time with my criminally-minded clients can be therapeutic not only because compared to theirs, my own life suddenly looks a picture of perfection, but also because of their readiness to laugh no matter how unfortunate their current circumstances might be to an outside observer.

This trait has never been more prominent than during a recent two-week trial in a sleepy seaside town. The trial was a four-hander, court jargon meaning there were four defendants, with multiple charges of assault and perverting the course of justice on the indictment, so not terribly trivial, not by a long stretch.

A word of context. Once upon a time, in the land of pre-Brexit Britain, rumour was doing rounds among Polish immigrants, supported by the Daily Mail, who else, which claimed that a number of Polish prisons had ran a campaign whereby they put up posters enticing prisoners to go to the UK, and start a new life in the said seaside town on completion of serving their sentences. What I have learnt about everyday reality in the town seems to suggest that, unfortunately, there might have been a grain of truth in the story and it is possible that more than a few Polish ex-convicts had taken up the offer.

Over the last few weeks I had an opportunity, I stop short of calling it a pleasure, to meet a large portion of the town's Polish community. This is what I learnt about their lives and crimes.

One of the first conclusions I had come to about their lifestyle was that their preferred source of income was blackmailing each other, followed by intimidation and extortion if deemed necessary. Victims were usually selected from among less clued-up members of their own community.

One day last week, half way through the trial, I asked a rather large group of cousins, neighbours and casual acquaintances who had been loyally present at court to show support for the defendants every single day, how come they were able to take so much time off work to be at court. After the roaring laughter subsided, I was told, 'Who is working? Work is for the weak and for newcomers, Miss. Nobody else has much time for work'.

They all know one another. The web of connections and inter-relations might sound impenetrable to an outsider, but they all seem to manoeuvre around it with ease. Any new Pole who arrives in town usually comes to join their brother-in-law, cousin, or their sister's ex-husband who have been settled there for a while. Each new arrival brings as much of their Polish home comforts across the English Channel as practicable, and whatever is too bulky to carry on their backs, they import to one of seven local Polish delicatessen shops later on.

They all visit one another all the time, with effervescence and generosity of spirit. It really does take the village to bring up the children.

Doused in vodka and beer, social life flourishes. All-nighters at friends' or neighbours' house are all part of everyday routine. Conversation topics might include debating comparative merits of a local prison versus Wandsworth prison in London. A number of the town's Poles have seen the inside of both establishments, Wandsworth being the UK authorities' prison of choice for detainees awaiting extradition, an experience several of the town's residents are familiar with.

At the end of the night, it is not unusual for regular party goers to end up having casual sex with relative strangers, or their lawfully wedded wife's cousin, or next-door neighbour's daughter. This carries an obvious risk of straining relationships when inebriation subsides, and can easily escalate into unpleasant incidents in the future. It is equally possible to make a spontaneous drunken decision to walk up to a mate's uncle's house with a crowbar at two thirty in the morning to teach him a lesson because he had been seen flirting with somebody's brother's girlfriend a couple of days earlier.

This type of spontaneous violent confrontation does not always come to fruition, because I am told that sometimes the intruders who arrive at the house with markedly hostile intentions of sorting out the said amorous uncle, might find their resolve crumble at the sight of a bottle of vodka on the table at the house of the intended victim.

On occasion, aggression does erupt, and a totally unnecessary, alcohol-fuelled violent incidents follow. Exactly what happens and why makes little sense afterwards to the perpetrators, the victims, the police and witnesses alike. Over the following few days an intricate damage limitation plot develops, with the aim of persuading witnesses and complainants to retract or alter original statements made to the police in the immediate aftermath of the incident. More often than not this is a complicated group effort whose logic is almost impossible to follow at trial.

Attempts to persuade witnesses to withdraw or amend their statements occasionally lead to charges of perverting the course of justice, which typically carries a sentence of up to two years imprisonment according to sentencing guidelines. A while ago a crown court judge significantly exceeded these guidelines and handed out a sentence of six years custody in one such case, a possible attempt to deter others from perpetuating such behaviour. To this day every Pole in town over the age of twelve is still able to quote excerpts from the judge's sentencing notes.

After listening to live evidence for three days, I had learnt that a typical Polish community way of interfering with witnesses goes somewhat like this;
Piotrek calls Karol, who is a good mate of Radek's who owes a favour to Michal from way back, and so he asks Dariusz to try and persuade Marcin, who is Beata's best friend, to take him to Szymon's place, where Magda and Norbert are already waiting for everybody, just to find out what can be done to calm things down somehow. Easy when you know how.

By the time the case finally goes to trial, witnesses change their stories, amend statements, swap sides, or prudently return to Poland just in case things get really nasty later on.

After months of preparations, trial begins. Each indictment against Polish inhabitants of our sleepy town reads almost exactly the same; the substantive charge of aggravated burglary, assault, or battery, followed by blackmail, threatening behaviour, threats to kill, harassment, witness intimidation.

There are four defendants and two interpreters. When my colleague and I introduce ourselves, the defendants are a little surprised at this dynamic, they expected an interpreter each, but are happy to share. One of them suggests a secret ballot whereby they state their preference as to who has the services of which interpreter, but other replies that this might make lady interpreters upset, if the voting goes strongly against one of them. Political correctness had not entered their world. The comment introduces the light-hearted tone to our relationship, and this is how it remains throughout the trial. Bearing in mind that on conviction these men face potentially double figures in prison, their cheerful mood is hard to understand, but it does help matters run smoothly for all of us.

Hour upon endless hour we listen to stories of drunken brawls and sexual indiscretions, as remembered by everybody who attended the party. Slight discrepancies are always to be expected, but in this case, it feels like I am listening to a totally different story from one witness' account to the next, each version affected by the amount of alcohol consumed by each of them on the night.

The key issue in this particular trial boils down to the question whether, when Dawid, having consumed eight pints of beer and half a litre of vodka, said to Magda that Przemek, her boyfriend, had better watch his back or he might soon be pushing up daisies, did Magda have reasonable grounds to suspect that Dawid genuinely intended to carry out the unequivocal threat that the phrase conveyed.

Our trial is in its third week. Each defendant and each witness require an interpreter. Each has their own barrister, as conflict of interest is rife in cases of this nature, it is neighbour against neighbour, cousin against cousin. Defendants change their stories, lawyers argue moot points of law with the judge in the absence of the jury, snow falls on tracks causing further delays. A huge amount of time and effort is spent to work out what really happened on that one fateful night months before, when somebody felt a surge of superhuman vibe and so instead of falling asleep under the table at the end of the party like everybody else, he decided to conquer the neighbourhood equipped with a crowbar and a set of spanners.

Naturally, not all Poles in this town are drunken hooligans, and aspiring career criminals. There are some honest, hardworking people among local immigrant population too, and such generalisations are grossly unfair to them. I would like to take this opportunity and apologise sincerely to all three of them.

When Love Goes Wrong

Making Sense of Domestic Violence

It was not long after I first started dealing with crime that I was introduced to domestic violence. It was a shock to discover how widespread it is, and it was a tough one for me to work out initially. I was at loss how to talk about it, how to make sense of it. My first and biggest hurdle used to be why do these women stay with their abusers, why don't they leave at the first sign of trouble? I worked with several women who had stayed with their boyfriends, husbands, and partners despite these men repeatedly breaking every rule of a happy family life if not quite every bone in their bodies. Women who I never believed even existed before I met them. Women who stayed with boyfriends whose drunken antics cost them long term custody of their children, who beat them so badly they miscarried, who slept with most of their friends, and who took most of their money. The more women who didn't leave I met the less black and white it was. They stayed for a multitude of reasons. They stayed because he was a good father, because he earned all the money, because it was his house, and they had nowhere to go, because their family liked him, because he threatened to take the children away, because they loved him, because he was their husband, because they could not imagine how they would cope without him, because they did not know the first thing about living on their own, because the worst husband was still better than no husband where they came from.

With time I came to accept that some women were never going to leave no matter what. I learnt a lot from these women over the years.

Lesson number one is that domestic abuse always happens to bad women. Women who make bad choices, who are bad mothers, bad cooks, bad drivers, bad companions, bad lovers, bad housewives. They are, as their abusers will make them believe, the ones ultimately responsible for the abuse. They are bringing it onto themselves. They ask for it by nagging, asking for things, being needy, by putting on weight and letting themselves go after having children, by wanting to be loved. By daring to comment on the abuser's family, work friends, or by not being entertaining enough at social occasions. The list is virtually endless, with infinite permutations, so it is impossible for a victim of abuse to try and protect herself against it by covering all bases. Her being alive, and being a woman, having opinions, feelings, needs and weaknesses is usually enough for her abuser to strike.

With time victims begin to believe that they deserve everything they get. They come to expect the abuse, they learn to live with it; they accept it as part of the everyday. They learn to put up a happy face for the children; their friends and family often have no idea what is really going on in their seemingly perfect lives. They learn to enjoy the tense silences between themselves and the abuser as moments of respite. Silence is good, silence means that the shouting and the anger is at bay, for now.

They try to pinpoint the exact moment when it all started. They search the history of their relationships, they recall first romantic dates, holding hands, laughing, those amazing first days, weeks, months. Is it possible that that was them, so dizzy with happiness, so hopeful and trusting, building castles for their future in the sand? When did it all start to crumble? Was it as early as her first pregnancy, when he started feeling overwhelmed with the new responsibilities? Was it when he got passed over for promotion, or didn't get that dream job and somehow, it became her fault? Was it when he started drinking heavily and that, naturally, was her fault too? Was it when he lost his job, because how could he have kept it, with all the pressure and the stress she put him under, and the children always demanding his attention as soon as he got home, and why were the children still up anyway, he deliberately stayed out late, so he didn't have to deal with them, day in day out. It started about then.

And so, it goes on, argument after argument, month after month, year after another unhappy year. All confined to their four walls, the children the only desperate witnesses. Desperate for it to stop, but equally desperate for the family to stay together.

In the absence of black eyes and bruises, compounded by willing concealment by all parties, the abuse can go undetected for, well, for ever really.

If and when professionals finally intervene, they encounter broken human beings, shadows of their former selves, they deal with women who doubt everything, who have no confidence in their looks, their parenting skills, their thoughts, and ideas. They often wonder whether their children would be better off if they were dead. They only know one thing; they are bad women. They know it with rock-solid certainty, because domestic abuse always happens to bad women.

Lesson number two is that there is never an excuse for abuse.

Domestic abuse can stay invisible to the outside world for a very long time, sometimes for a lifetime, its sounds perfectly muffled by the four walls of despair, fear, weakness and pride.

It is an insidious killer. It inflicts irreparable wounds to the heart, but the heart does not stop, despite victims' frequent desperate prayers that it would. That it would stop. That everything would stop.

Instead, it carries on. Everything carries on for another day, and another, as if nothing happened. It is quiet for a while, and the victim dares to hope, to smile, to laugh even. Until it happens again. It will always happen again. She never learns this simple truth. She tries to cheer herself up by remembering the good times, there used to be good times, right? She keeps hoping for a miracle, for him to go back to being the kind loving husband and father she still remembers him being, once, surely, she remembers this correctly? He must have been kind and loving once, right? This memory is fading with every new outburst of uncontrolled anger, with torrent of verbal abuse, designed to hurt, to degrade, to break.

She keeps quiet about it. She denies it when asked about it, she denies it most of all to herself. She feels ashamed and embarrassed, she feels exactly how he wants her to feel. She does not report any incidents to the police, she stays at home for days waiting for her bruises to heal.

I meet her at a family court hearing to decide the extent and form of her contact with children. Yes, her contact with her children. It turns out the abuse was not as silent as she thought. Neighbours called the police, social services got involved, children were placed with a foster family. Without children her whole life collapsed, literally. Without children she was no longer entitled to benefits, so rent arrears, and eviction followed. Fast forward to self-harming, addiction to pain killers, alcohol abuse, a budding cocaine habit.

With a whole army of other people, we are hard at work trying to put pieces of her broken life together again. Looking at her vacant face, her all-pervading misery we all think the same thought. There is no excuse for this. There is no excuse. There. Is. No. Excuse.

Love Conquers All

Domestic abuse is always sad and it brings misery among all involved, this much is not in dispute, but like with so many things in life, not everything is always black and white. Some couples clearly cannot live with, but equally cannot stay away, from each other. They muddle through, some time together, some time apart, year after year, their lives punctuated by big bust-ups and fragile truces. Neither of them ready to walk away, they never tire of attempts to find a way to make it work. Today I am a witness to one such ongoing drama.

A restraining order might seem an unlikely aphrodisiac to an objective observer.

And yet... My experiences as a court interpreter point out repeatedly to the fact that common sense and logic are often all but abandoned on entering the world of relationships marred with domestic violence and family court proceedings and today is no different.

Robert faces two breaches of a restraining order and criminal damage. These are the charges Robert reluctantly pleaded guilty to at the previous hearing. He had spent the last 7 weeks in prison awaiting the sentence. This in itself sounds like an overkill on somebody's part. Since entering his guilty plea, he has also been expecting a probation officer to visit him in prison to prepare a pre-sentence report (PSR) as ordered by the court. Today we meet via video link in a very cramped room at a suburban court house. The picture is blurred and I cannot work out Robert's facial expressions, but his tone conveys exasperation and confusion. The fact that the probation officer never turned up to interview him in prison does not surprise anybody too much. A glitch in the system, clearly, but before the solicitor can say "application to adjourn", the judge starts flicking through pages and pages of the case history. It all begins to unravel.

- How old are your children, Robert?

- 4, 3 and a 5 months old baby, Your Honour, judge, sir.

- Which means that the baby was conceived when the restraining order was already in place, is that correct?

- It looks that way, doesn't it? And sir, judge, she tells me she might be pregnant again.

After that it becomes borderline farcical.

The judge rules that based on the circumstances and undeniable facts in the matter, which lie before him, there is no realistic prospect for the restraining to ever be effective. Instead, he imposes a rather impossible order forbidding the defendant from using aggressive, threatening, offensive words or behaviour towards the complainant. Indefinitely. As in for ever. From this day forward. I mean, come on....? Not even the strictest, most solemn sounding wedding vows demand *'and I shall not raise my voice to you until death do us part.'*

District Judge X sitting at court house today believes however that this is a fair and proportionate sentence to impose on Robert. He lifts a restraining order, but by imposing a good behaviour order, he puts an additional strain on this couple's already troubled relationship. Just think about it. Does a good behaviour order really encourage a frank and honest relationship, is Robert ever going to dare speak his mind about the quality of his partner's cooking, her weight, her parenting skills or anything else that matters? Not if he wishes to be spared another stint in prison.

All things considered, I cannot make up my mind whether the judge's decision was a stroke of judiciary genius, or unrealistic wishful thinking, making a difficult situation impossible. The level of interference this order allows for sits uneasily with me, but then again, perhaps it's a case of desperate situation calling for desperate measures? Let's see how this would work in my own marriage. My husband would have to stay super calm and, well-mannered and attentive, so I had no reason to think that he was being rude, bad-tempered or neglectful, which would make him in breach of the order and lead us straight back into that courtroom. Mind you, I like to think that I would not allow myself to get entangled in anything even remotely resembling this scenario in the first place. I find the love is blind notion as appealing as the next person, but surely it is not deaf and mute at the same time.

Later that night over dinner my husband looks me straight in the eye and tells me that the chicken is a bit dry. I want to kiss him and I beam back at him with joy, we have a strong and healthy marriage.

Communication Gap

My interpreting days do not always go smoothly, and whenever they don't, the first thing I do is question my ability to facilitate communications between parties separated by language. This in turn makes me wonder what causes the difficulties in smoothing out the bumps and imperfections in encounters between service providers and their clients. Cultural differences go a long way towards explaining it, but sometimes it feels that total lack of insight on client's part and their thinly disguised contempt for the system in which, for one reason or another, they have got themselves tangled up are the main stumbling blocks.

Today I meet with a court appointed independent social worker to conduct a so-called section 7 interview with a father who has made a child arrangement application to court wishing to re-establish contact with his son whom he has not seen for several months. Family courts request a Section 7 report whenever there are concerns that parental application might compromise a child's safety and wellbeing and might therefore not be in the child's best interest.

The father comes across as not the brightest and on edge as soon as we meet. Just some things he says. The social worker stays professional, and manages to maintain cheerful smile and indifference throughout.

The father does not understand why the court might have concerns. What kind of concerns, anyway, what do you mean concerns, where is all this coming from? His only concern is that his son might not recognise him after all this time, because the child mother kept him from having any contact for so long out of pure spite. Yes, the police attended occasionally, but his ex- always withdrew all allegations the next day each time so what's the big deal for Pete's sake. Swapping a much stronger expletive for Pete at the last moment is not lost on anyone. He paid voluntary maintenance above and beyond the statutory amount until she stopped contact, so what's the problem.

He bought expensive Christmas presents, which he describes to us in great details, including price tags, were they passed on to his son? He is willing to resume payments if she allows him contact again, but this time he is not going to be stupid and will only pay exactly what he is obliged to by law, because he is not going to be made look like an idiot. The social worker explains politely that this is not about money, maintenance or presents, but about his child's safety in the view of historical domestic violence. He shifts in his seat, tightens his fist, clenches his jaw, but then decides to soften his face with a grin and denies any domestic violence, and says that he is really looking forward to the next court hearing and after that seeing his son again, he has already bought him lots of toys for when he can see him next, and he is willing to resume maintenance payments as soon as regular contact is established, but not before, he is not going to pay for nothing, he is not an idiot. Not being seen as an idiot seems particularly important to him, so he asserts that he is not an idiot several times during the interview. The social worker and I still have our doubts. The interview continues in this vein for a while longer, the father brings up maintenance and expensive gifts every few minutes, the social worker counters it patiently with details of domestic abuse against the child's mother, stressing that this is the only topic the court is concerned about at this stage.

We are light years away from any sort of insight, or understanding of the issue on father's side. Perhaps I am an idiot myself for thinking naively, that my interpreting skills can break all communication barriers between the two parties I am here to assist.

Crown Court - When It Gets Really Serious

The Interpretation of Murder

Murder stays with you. It pulls you in. It changes you.

You sit next to him in the dock, day in day out.

He sees you as the closest thing he has had to a friend for a long time. You are also the only person with whom he can express himself freely in his own language. For most of the day you provide a clearly defined service which allows for the smooth and efficient execution of justice. But life in the dock is not all about smooth and efficient execution of justice. It is also about endless waiting time whilst technicians test video links, teams of barristers assemble their accoutrements, and judges take their time to arrive. Plenty of time to chat.

It starts as inconsequential small talk about prison food and traffic on the way from prison, but before you know it you are listening to stories of deprived childhood, of broken home, of unbelievable poverty, of years spent lacking almost everything, years of envy, anger, greed, and then inevitable fall into crime, petty at first, growing bigger and bolder, becoming the way of life, getting out of hand.

You listen to the stories because a part of you wants to find an excuse for him, to justify his actions, to understand.

This is a dangerous path to follow, but what's the alternative? Say nothing at all for eight long weeks except what you are paid to say? Sit arm in arm with a six-foot two man and ignore his presence except to whisper court proceedings to him in the language he understands? Impossible. So you hear yourself say hello, how are you? You smile out of habit. And before you know it, you are back in the same conversation, back where you left off at 4.30 the day before.

Once you start feeling sorry for him, with his alcoholic mother, father unknown, his joyless empty life, you are walking into a trap, eyes wide open. Small talk in the dock can obscure the facts sometimes.

One thing in particular stays with you longer than you would wish, *'I'd done bad things in my life, I steal for a living for God's sake, but not this, murder takes something else, something I don't have within me'*.

People say a lot of things, don't they?

By week three you know quite a lot about him. All he knows about you is your name.

His barristers ask you to translate text messages retrieved from his phone in case he was careless about something to somebody in the last twelve months.

You trawl through hundreds of texts and you find nothing relevant to the case, but you stumble upon several clumsily poetic declarations of love to a nameless girl. You feel uncomfortable, snooping on his private life like this. Next time you see him, you look for a vulnerability that you had not suspected existed. He does not know you have read his messages. You do not tell him. Trial continues.

You see the victim's parents coming into court for the first time. You feel awkward. After all, you share the language with the defendants. What if the family sees you as connected somehow to the evil that destroyed their world? You know that thought is irrational but you think it nonetheless. So, you just acknowledge them with a solemn silent nod every time you see them. Which is every day, they return every day.

The time comes for your client to give evidence. Three long gruelling days of relentless questions, his long-winded convoluted answers when he tries to offer an explanation where there simply isn't one. Lies, and more blatant lies, punctuated by nervous sips of water.

Cross-examination, and the steely eyes of the prosecutor when he says, the truth is *Mr… that you, jointly with your co-defendants, did plan to kill him, you did plan to dispose of his body and you made sure…*

A short break, you go outside the courtroom, nobody speaks. The wigged barristers, the police officers, the usher, the whole entourage. You take a deep breath and you bite your lips. This is more than you have ever bargained for. Your eyes fill up with tears against your best efforts to keep it professional. And then the victim's mother, an old woman dressed in black with straggly grey hair comes up to you, puts her hand on your shoulder and whispers almost inaudibly, 'you are doing well, you are doing a good job, child', and the tears just flowed.

'All parties in the case of…' we are being called back in.

When the trial is over and they are taken away to start serving their life sentences for murder, conspiracy to rob and a string of minor offences, you walk away from it all for the last time, but you are not free. You catch the train home, you sit by the window and you watch familiar sights of the city around you, but your mind is drifting back, you replay random moments from the last two months in your head, you go over the evidence, you rewind to when the pathologist said, *no, my findings are not conclusive, but they are based on the process of elimination…*

Then you jump to the fibre expert evidence, and one by one you slowly peel off all the fibres found on the body all over again. You reconstruct the last few hours of the body's life. Because the victim was always just a body to you. No matter how hard you tried, you could not make it come back alive in your imagination. It remained firmly on the floor of its living room where it was found two days after death, bruised and abandoned, stripped of clothes and all dignity.

Murder stays with you, it pulls you in, it changes you. You hope this does not mean a life sentence for you too.

Changing Lives, One Word at a Time

Walking home from a tube station today I find myself thinking, *I saved this guy from prison today*. On the great scale of things, the degree of influence I exerted over the order of universe this morning was negligible, but from the point of view of my client, Piotr, I was a fairy godmother, Superwoman and Buffy rolled into one.

I arrived at court nice and early. Piotr was there already, young, nervous, fidgety and very Polish. His barrister was running late. I was watching him without interest, sipping my Costa and flicking through the Metro absent-mindedly, pretending to be just about anybody else, except who I was, his interpreter. You see, sometimes I just don't feel like making small talk with my client, all I want to do is my job, which is 'facilitating communication between a member of criminal justice system and a non-English speaker'. Piotr was being very popular with his friends and family in the meantime. He received numerous phone calls, all in Polish, which he was cutting short with 'cool, thanks, still waiting, will do, bye'. Half an hour later his barrister sashayed in, her robe flapping, wig slightly askew. We found a quiet room and started the conference. As an interpreter I am thrown right in the middle of a drama series, a life changing mistake, a tragedy. I am trying to piece the full story together quickly from morsels of information, picking up clues on the way. This time there were two charges; a burglary and an attempted burglary, but, as the barrister explained, seen as a part of one continuous activity. The victim assessed the value of stolen goods at £7,000 but the totality of items actually found on Piotr was one Michael Kors scarf. According to Piotr, he was very drunk at the time. He needn't even have said that, this is always, but I mean always the case. He was walking along after a heavy night out, when he noticed an open door, so he went in, took a scarf and a handbag from the house, no, he really didn't know why he took those items, and then he left. A few minutes later he panicked and threw away the handbag somewhere along the way. He might have had a cigarette while in the property, he couldn't be sure now, what does it matter, anyway?

This was the downstairs flat, which, according to him, had already been broken into when he entered it. There was also an upstairs flat in the property, and the police believed that whoever broke to the downstairs flat, also attempted to break into the upstairs flat, but abandoned the project, having smashed the window and kicked the front door a couple of times. No other suspects were apprehended. Piotr was found not far from the property, detained, arrested, interviewed, charged with the burglary of the downstairs flat and attempted burglary of the upstairs flat, and then bailed to court. He pleaded guilty to the burglary on a previous occasion, today was his PCMH (plea and case management hearing) in relation to the attempted burglary, which he was consistently denying. Well, actually, not exactly consistently. During police interview he lied, according to what he was saying today, and admitted both offences. He then changed his story and was now claiming that he had not gone near the upstairs flat at all. Today the plan was to maintain the non-guilty plea to the attempted burglary charge and to confirm trial date later this month.

As the conference progressed and the barrister was completing trial preparation forms it became obvious that Piotr was not following the ins and outs of the court procedure, but he insisted that he was not going to plead guilty to the attempted burglary because he did not do it. The barrister was not advising for or against. She must have already resigned herself to losing the trial, as Piotr was likely to be found guilty by the jury. The lying to the police, or in any event changing the version of events from the police interview to the court hearing never looks good.

The words of police caution recited thousand times over each day at police station across the land, 'you do not have to say anything, but it may harm your defence if you do not mention while questioned something you will later rely on in court' do come to haunt many a hapless criminal. It really does what it says on the tin. If a defendant changes their story between their first police interview and the trial, they really are in a bit of a pickle, the court does take it very much against them.

Piotr was only interested in one subject now. Is it definitely going to be a prison sentence if found guilty after the trial and how long for; the answers were most likely yes, and between 12 and 18 months. This news upset Piotr greatly. He welled up and was visibly shaken. Because you see, his brother is getting married in May, and this would mean missing the wedding, and they were very close with his brother, and the whole family was going to be there and … his voice broke, and tears flowed. He didn't care about anything else, but the date was set, the reception booked, invitations sent out, and it was going to be the highlight of his year and now he was going to miss it.

We finished the conference, the barrister disappeared in the courtroom, and we stayed outside. Piotr resumed his fidgeting and his endless telephone conversations, I opened my book, happy to wait our turn for however long it took. We are paid by the hour you see.

But then something switched and the quiet reading went out of the window. I hate it when it happens. I try not to, but I knew I was getting involved, I kept thinking of this bloody May wedding and there was no use, I closed the book and thought let's see what can be done.

I started talking to Piotr, casually at first. I asked him if he had understood everything that we discussed so far and whether he knew what his options were. And then I had an idea, a possible solution, but I needed to steer him in the right direction and then make is seem that it was his idea all along. Interpreters are bound by rules of impartiality at all times, so we need to tread carefully. I told him that sometimes ('I had a similar case once…') it is possible to request that the judge indicates whether they would give a defendant a prison sentence should he plead guilty to all charges on all facts on that day. I was tempted to show off and say that this approach was called asking for a Goodyear indication, Goodyear being the name of a defendant in a case where it first came about, but I resisted. I further explained to him that he had nothing to lose, and if the judge said that he could not guarantee non-custodial sentence on full plea, then he could always maintain his original non-guilty plea and proceed to trial by jury.

Piotr liked that idea very much, so I called the barrister and briefly summarised that Piotr was keen to find out whether he would be going to prison if he decided to plead guilty today. Oh, I see, the barrister said, this is called a Goodyear indication (duh!) and even though it is not being practised as much as it used to, this case it actually a perfect candidate for it, as Piotr had already pleaded guilty to one charge. Leave it with me, let's see what I can do. To cut the rest of the story short, the judge agreed to Goodyear, indicated that taking all the circumstances into consideration he would just about be able to suspend the sentence today, Piotr was re-arraigned, pleaded guilty to both charges, the prosecutor, taken aback by the turn of events did not have any input, and Piotr walked out with a 12 months sentence, suspended for 2 years.

Piotr wanted to hug me and worse, he kept thanking me, rather than the barrister, to the latter's confusion, and he danced out of the court already on the phone to his brother telling him good news about the wedding.

I believe this is called a butterfly effect. Something about flapping wings on the other side of the globe and causing a dramatic change in the course of events. If only I'd packed the latest unputtable down Robert Galbraith yarn this morning and not David Cameron's biography, Piotr would definitely be missing the wedding.

And finally, what I did today should not have happened. As an interpreter I should have stayed impartial and indifferent at all times and not engage in the dramas I witness in the course of my interpreting services. Theoreticians of my field, fantasists are also another good word for them, believe that a live interpreter with a heartbeat should come as close to resembling a translation machine as possible, without any of the machine's shortcomings such as not recognising the context or tripping over grammar.

So, I guess by departing from these rules I failed to be the best interpreter I could be, but I like to think that I didn't.

Floater

Last Monday morning I had settled into an uneventful day of telephone interpreting when an email came, at 11.50am with, as soon as you can please, local Crown Court job request. The job details said 'Trial', always a good catch. Adrenaline got me to court in under half an hour. The trial was a floater, which meant we did not have a courtroom allocated and were just hanging in there in the hope that another trial might prove ineffective, and then we would jump in in its place.

The defendant was in custody, we went to see him in the cells, and explained to him, that after lunch we might get lucky and get a room, so his trial might start, but then again, we might not. He looked at us blankly, trying to work out whether we were serious, or just having a laugh, an in-joke he was not privy to. After lunch we went to the listings office and watched two people stare at their computer screens for a long time, they squinted hard, and shook heads. Nope, sorry, nothing seems to be available today. We went to see the defendant again, and explained to him the idea behind a floating trial, or a floater. Courts habitually double or triple book themselves, in the knowledge, bases on everyday experience that some trials fall through on the first day, thus freeing the courtroom and the judge to deal with another matter. There are many reasons why a trial might prove ineffective at the last moment. The defendant might lose their nerve and plead guilty on the day. Key prosecution witnesses might not turn up. The defendant, if on bail, might not turn up. Statistically speaking, these occurrences are frequent enough to justify the introduction of a floater, a judicial reserves bench. We told our defendant that unfortunately we would not be starting his trial today, as there was no room for us. He once again looked at us with incredulity, before he finally asked, as calmly as the situation allowed, so why was I brought here first thing in the morning, to beat the traffic, only to spend seven hours on the hard piece of wooden bench, and to be taken back to prison without stepping foot in the courtroom? We had no answer for him beyond, this is how the system works, or not, nothing we can do about it, so we shall see you again tomorrow, ok?

Except, we didn't.

By the time I got home, there was an email from my agency letting me know that the trial had been cancelled by the court, so I did not need to attend on Tuesday.

This was a bit odd, as I had said my goodbye-see you tomorrow to everybody at court an hour before. So, I called the court listings office just to be sure. I was informed that yes, unfortunately, the trial had to be cancelled at this very short notice, because another trial had overrun and there was no prospect of us getting a room on Tuesday, and we would have to take one day at a time, very sorry about that.

My Tuesday ended up pretty full on, with last minute booking for out of town in the morning and a short-written translation, also last minute, after that.

As I rushed through the final spellcheck, my thoughts wandered off towards the defendant, and how his Tuesday might have been. Pure guesswork, but with a degree of experience-based confidence. When he woke up to get ready for court, he was told, by a guard speaking loud and slow with lots of hand and arm gestures to aid understanding, that there would be NO ... COURT ... TODAY. NO COURT, OK? UNDERSTAND?

This left the defendant to spend the rest of the day confused as to what happened, and why. He tried calling his solicitors, but he did not get through.

I was ready to file the case away as one of those things, but then, the agency called that I was requested to attend court on Wednesday, one-hour hearing, same case. I accepted out of curiosity more than anything, as one-hour booking makes very little financial sense to a freelance interpreter.

Wednesday brought an unexpected end to the case. Sometime between Monday evening and Wednesday morning, in a sensational twist, the prosecution decided to drop the sexual assault charge. The complainant, after reviewing the CCTV footage afresh, was no longer willing to give evidence on the sexual aspect of the offence. This left the sole remaining charge on the indictment of assault by beating, which, at its highest point amounted to the defendant 'unlawfully placing his hand in the complainant's hip area'. The defendant had already pleaded guilty to plain assault early on in the case. Why was this eleventh hour decision by the prosecution sensational? Let's see.

The defendant was arrested on a warrant issued by a court in another part of the country, for failure to surrender to court on an allegation of a low-level criminal damage. Following his arrest, the plan was to keep him in police custody overnight and transfer him to the court the following day to deal with the matter.

The incident we were dealing with now took place at the police custody suite as he was being escorted to the cells by a female police officer.

He was drunk at the time, which never helps. It was alleged that he looked at the officer's breasts and asked her if she 'fancied a shag?' He says he didn't even know what that word meant. He still pronounces it 'shack'. It was further alleged that he placed his hand on the police officer's hip. The allegation ended there.

The defendant accepted, albeit reluctantly, the assault part of the incident, but vehemently denied any sexual intention. At that stage the prosecution was not prepared to drop the sexual nature of the allegation, and trial preparation began.

Because of his history of failure to surrender to court on previous occasion, the defendant was denied bail. He had spent the intervening six months in custody awaiting the trial, which brings us back to our floater on Monday.

By Wednesday, as the prosecution dropped the sexual part of the allegation all that remained for the court to do was to sentence the defendant in relation to the assault by beating. The judge, the prosecutor and the defence barrister all made awkward speeches about how badly this case had been managed, and how it was a disgrace that the defendant had served the equivalent of one-year imprisonment, awaiting his trial on the charge that was now no longer pursued by the prosecution. The judge formally acquitted him of sexual assault, and sentenced him to a one hundred pounds fine or one day in prison in case of non-payment for the assault by beating.

The defendant was an unassuming man, by now completely and utterly resigned to accept whatever was being thrown at him, convinced that everything in life conspired to bring the greatest misery upon him that any given set of circumstances could create at any given moment. As it dawned on him that he had just spent six months in prison for touching a police officer's hip, in a non-sexual manner, as was formally confirmed today, he cried tears of powerless frustration.

At the end of the hearing the prosecutor hurriedly gathered his stuff, and as he scurried to the door, he turned round and said to nobody in particular, please do not mention to anybody that I did this case. I know exactly how he felt.

Courtroom Drama Nitty-Gritty

Somewhere-in-London Crown Court, Application to Vacate Plea Hearing, time estimate half a day.

As usual I am the first among the interested parties to arrive, so I sit outside court 10 and wait. Three grumpy solicitors arrive together and plonk themselves beside me. What they say makes little sense, they seem rather nervous and keep flicking through pages and pages of typed up statements and handwritten notes.

They ask me if I am the Polish interpreter in the case of Daniel so and so. Yes, I reply ready for a friendly chat, and ask them if they are his defence team. 'Not any more', hisses one of them, 'his barrister will be with you soon'. Okay, then. Attempts at small talk abandoned, I wait on.

Larger than life barrister arrives and we go to the cells to talk to Daniel. I have a vague recollection of dealing with both of them before on the day his trial was supposed to start, but was 'proved ineffective', I cannot recall the reason for this now. As the conference progresses, it all comes back into focus.

Daniel arrived in London 7 months ago. Three days later he managed to get lost in the underbelly of South London. Not having a bank account as yet in this country, he carried all his money, several hundred pounds, in a wallet in his trouser pocket. We are not here to judge the wisdom of his personal security choices, so we do not dwell on this. He got on a bus and attempted to pay for his ticket taking out a £50 note from a thick wad of fifties and twenties. The bus driver told him where to go. He got off. He noticed that another man, who got on the bus just behind him had now hopped off too. This planted a suspicion in Daniel's mind that the man intended to rob him. When the man then followed Daniel to another bus stop and, according to Daniel, brushed against him, it was confirmation enough and at this point Daniel punched the man in the chest. A single punch, as he maintains. The other man fell to the ground and sustained multiple serious injuries, including fractured pelvis, fractured skull and brain haemorrhage. The victim turned out to be severely autistic, frail man. Daniel was arrested, interviewed and charged with section 18 and section 20 offences. Which is industry jargon for GBH with intent and GBH without intent respectively. GBH stands for grievous bodily harm- on conviction the two short words 'with intent' can add several years to the sentence.

From the word go Daniel was being advised by a firm of solicitors that, like everybody else in the story, shall of course remain anonymous. A solicitor who assisted him during police interview advised him early on not to answer any questions. This confused Daniel who was desperate to tell the police his version of events, which was that he punched this man in order to protect himself from being robbed. He maintained the same position throughout. He did not assault this man, did not attack him, he acted only to protect his property. He emphatically denied any intent to cause harm to the victim. He claimed the solicitors advised him that based on the extent of the victim's injuries he should plead not guilty to section 18 (with intent), but guilty to section 20 (without intent). At court he followed their advice, adding a basis of plea. Basis of plea is a kind of 'yes, but, no but' approach. I admit the offence, but not quite, not all of it and I am generally a nice person. The basis of plea needs to be put in writing and offered to the prosecution for them to consider whether they are happy to accept the basis of plea. If they do not accept the basis of plea, and they insist on acceptance of guilt on full facts, a trial date is set. Most of the time a lawyer writes up the basis of plea document and the defendant agrees it and signs.

Sometimes, quite often actually, defence are able to make a deal with the prosecution and if the defendant pleads guilty to one offence, the prosecution are prepared to remove the more serious charge and proceed to sentence the defendant only on what they pleaded to. In our case the prosecution did not accept Daniel's plea to section 20 on the basis and insisted on keeping section 18 offence on the indictment, so the trial date was set.

In the intervening months the solicitors visited Daniel in prison, went over details of the case with him and prepared his defence statement.

On the first day of trial his barrister went to the cells to say hello and to confirm the position.

Just to clarify, barristers often meet their clients for the first time on the day of trial. They are the big guns of justice throwing their weight around your TV in courtroom dramas, complete with moth-ridden wigs and other intimidating props. The case is prepared by a firm of solicitors, who then assign the job of representing the defendant in court to a barrister.

Daniel repeated his mantra that he only pushed or punched this guy once to protect his wallet as he genuinely thought that the victim was about to rob him.

And this is when the brown stuff hit the fan. The barrister asked Daniel, 'Just out of interest, why did you plead guilty to section 20 assault if you claim that you were acting in self-defence?'

Daniel shifted in his chair and said in a rather tired voice the line he had repeated endlessly in the recent months, that he did not assault anybody, he was just protecting his money. In the next twenty minutes the barrister patiently unravelled the case thread by thread and came up with new course of action for Daniel; sack your solicitors, as they did not give you correct advice on self-defence, waive the legal privilege in relation to the confidentiality of advice received, and then he, the barrister, will make an application to the court to vacate the guilty plea to give Daniel an opportunity to enter a not guilty plea to section 20 as he believed he acted in self-defence.

That was two months ago and here we are today, the barrister readying himself for battle against Daniel's previous solicitors. He is rearing to go, almost boyishly excited about the whole thing. He whispers to me, shaking his finger, you see the solicitors are pulling rank now, they all recently prepared statements claiming that they had fully advised Daniel on self-defence and the use of reasonable force. But they didn't, you see! They didn't! He literally jumps up and down. None of them mentioned it in in their attendance notes from court or notes taken during any of several conferences they held with Daniel! I am sure of it!

We go into court. The judge makes his displeasure with the barrister's application abundantly clear. The idea of putting a team of solicitors in a witness box so their professional judgement can be challenged by a defence counsel does not sit comfortably with him.

Daniel gives evidence first.

- What is your understanding of section 20 is and why did you plead guilty to it?

- I pleaded guilty because I hit the man.

- Did your lawyers explain the concept of self-defence to you at any stage?

- No.

- Did they explain the concept of reasonable force at any stage?

- No.

- Do you accept that you assaulted the victim?

- No.

- Did you intend to cause him any harm?

- No.

We break for lunch. The solicitors outside view me with suspicion. All a bit childish really.

In the afternoon the solicitors all give evidence. The barrister is grilling them on the lack of any reference to self-defence in any of their copious notes and documents prepared during all previous court hearings. He suggests that they did not advise Daniel properly in the case, and they denied him the option of running self-defence argument during his trial. They are all asked the same questions, all give more or less the same answers, which is that they did not see the need to write this up in the documentation but yes, they fully advised Daniel on self-defence, of course they did, as they always do. The judge clearly sides with the solicitors throughout. At some point he actually apologises for all the questions, and shouts at the barrister for trying to doubt the solicitors' professional integrity. This part of the early afternoon courtroom drama makes for very uncomfortable viewing. I wish for a commercial break.

The judge announces his decision. He starts by telling the barrister off for accusing the solicitors of unprofessional conduct. It all seems a foregone conclusion until, in a twist worthy of an episode of Silk, the judge picks up the, half forgotten by now, basis of plea document and says, 'there is however an ever so small criticism that can be extended to the content of this document, which makes it equivocal, and therefore I am obliged to give the defendant the benefit of the doubt, small as it is, and so I allow the application to vacate previous guilty plea'. Jaws drop, eyes open wide, silence in the courtroom.

Daniel gave up listening to the proceedings about an hour ago. I nudge him and repeat the result of today's hearing. He stares at me blankly. All of this overwhelms him. He responds to being re-arraigned in a daze. A new trial date is set and we wrap up for the day. Daniel's exhaustion rubs off on me.

The barrister catches up with me outside. His excitement unabated, he rambles incessantly, giving his interpretation of today's events; you see, judges don't like exposing solicitors as incompetent, so he picked a totally inconsequential argument, limiting his criticism of their action to the drafting of one document, because he wasn't going in a million years agree with me even though it was obvious he agreed with me, blah blah blah. I began to drift.

Today felt like a good day. Too drained to come up with a clever punchline to the events of the day, I just enjoy the anti-climax, the tiredness and the warm afternoon breeze as I walk away from them.

I never did find out what happened to Daniel in the end. This is just how the system works. One interpreter works during the preliminary hearing, another interpreter is booked for the trial, and yet another for sentencing.

Trials and Tribulations

IQ testing should be me made compulsory before a defendant is allowed to insist on having a crown court trial. I am still working on an exact wording of the petition to this effect, watch this space. Until this is implemented, there will be regular occurrences where twenty odd people gather in a courtroom for six hours a day, for a trial lasting a week at the very least, wasting public time and money.

GBH with intent (Grievous Bodily Harm, contrary to section 18 of the Offences Against the Person Act, 1861) is a serious charge and on conviction carries a lengthy custodial sentence. That was, I believe, the totality of what the defendant understood about the case against him. Phrases such as overwhelming strength of prosecution evidence and adverse inference had no chance of penetrating deeply enough into his consciousness to have an impact on his way of thinking.

His defence statement might as well have been abbreviated to 'I didn't do it'. He is not particularly troubled by the fact that this flies in the face of pretty conclusive CCTV footage evidence and corroborated by two key prosecution witnesses, one of them being the victim and the other the defendant's ex-partner and the mother of his child.

The incident occurred at an address the defendant was prohibited from attending by a domestic violence prevention order issued a few weeks previously, which clearly suggests history of, well, domestic violence, but we are directed by the judge not to speculate, as it is irrelevant to the current case. He claims had no idea that order was in place, so surely, he couldn't be blamed from breaking it. Being told that yes, he could be, annoys him greatly.

He claims that somebody else must have caused the serious injuries he stands accused of inflicting. Somebody who was already in the flat when he got there or another somebody who came in as he was leaving.

We watched the CCTV again in court today and it shows that nobody else entered the block of flats during relevant time, or within four hours before or after the incident. He shouts, quite angry now, 'I didn't do it, how many times do I need to say this, and I did not smash his head with no frying pan, not me, man'. The barrister is way too long in the tooth to be in any way perturbed by this outburst and asks calmly, 'well if you didn't, who did?' The defendant decides to answer this and all the questions that follow with short and sweet, 'no idea', which speeds up our conference considerably.

In the light of what I have heard and observed of the defendant during the first couple of days, I go out of my way to be as polite and respectful to him as I possibly can, just in case he loses his temper when I sit next to him.

Three days later.

I underestimated my client. He invents a new variation of the previous version of his defence every day, sometimes dexterously changing his account between the beginning and end of one conference with his barrister. 'Another guy was there as I was leaving, there was another guy there when I arrived, my ex opened the door, the complainant opened the door. He spoke to me, he didn't speak to me, as I was leaving, he was having an argument with somebody in the flat, somebody on the phone, I think his name was Robert, his name might have been Andrzej. There was one more person in the flat, there were two other men there, I don't know, I can't remember.'

The barrister is looking increasingly desperate, murderous and suicidal in turns.

On day four the defendant announces triumphantly that he had now made a decision to 'tell the truth' when he gives evidence. He looks really pleased with himself and expects our approval. This pushes the barrister over the edge, 'I don't deal in truth!' he shouts, 'I act on your instructions, which change every time I see you'. If you change your instructions again by next week, after I asked the prosecution witnesses questions based on your previous set of instructions, it will make me professionally embarrassed and I will have great difficulty representing you any further.

Barristers are hired by solicitors to represent their clients in court. They do not usually choose cases, so they have to work with whatever falls into their lap, and it usually falls there just a few days before the trial. Often, they see the defendant for the first time on the first day of trial. The case would have been prepared by the solicitors' office in the months leading to the trial, they would have met up with the defendant drafting and redrafting his defence statement and discussing the case, checking and double checking whether he might want to change his plea. The idea is that by the time trial begins, solicitors and the defendant would have agreed on final version of his defence and the barrister is then supposed to run with this version, no matter what their personal opinion about the plausibility of it is. If the defendant then changes his story again half way through the trial, motivated by, more often than not, a last ditch attempt to fit his defence around how the evidence has been unfolding, the barrister might decide at some point that he or she has had enough of that cat and mouse game, raise their hands in the air and shout 'Sorry, folks, I am professionally embarrassed, I am out of here'.

This made me think, and this is just an aside, that when a barrister declares himself professionally embarrassed, he walks away from the case, his head held high and his pride intact.

When an interpreter finds herself professionally embarrassed during a trial, this usually means she has a momentary total mental block in front of the jury and forgets the word *frying pan* in her own language. She hangs her head in shame and prays for the earth to swallow her whole. Horses for courses.

Monday morning, sixth day of the trial.

Defendant decided against putting forward a new version of 'truth', so we are running with his old 'truth', which means the barrister stays in the case, and is only as embarrassed as everybody else involved in defending this matter. Defendant gives evidence today, seemingly unfazed by the fact that he is able to answer very few of his own barrister's questions and almost none of the prosecutor's. I focus my efforts on saying, 'I don't know, I can't remember' for the umpteenth time without sounding like a robot.

By the time defendant finishes their performance in the witness box, there isn't that much left for barristers to do in the trial, so they use that time to explain categories of the offence and sentencing guidelines in relation to each category. We try to breach this subject with him today, but it is not easy.

- 'Why do you want to talk to me about this?'

- 'Because Mr X, based on the unassailable solidity of the evidence against you, I am not overly confident that the outcome of this case is going to be favourable to us'.

I bring down the barrister's soaring eloquence to the level the defendant is likely to understand. He looks genuinely confused, 'but why, I told them I didn't do it, didn't I?'

Day eight of original four. We have finally arrived at closing speeches today. We have also arrived at the Magistrates Court, as this trial has now overstayed its welcome at the city's Crown Court. Our judge is what is called a Recorder, which means he is a part time judge, and part time still practising barrister. He is doing his judging for a few months a year and for the rest of the year he is doing his defending and or prosecuting. Recorders are invited to sit on trials whenever there is a gap in regular court listings. Last week there was a five-day gap in the crown court so our trial was listed there with a four-day estimate, hoping to finish in three. Now that the trial has dragged its feet beyond usual level of delays, we have been relegated to the Magistrates Court, our gown and wig brigade looking ever so slightly out of place among the local drunken and disorderly crowd. We press on.

The jury took just over an hour to return a unanimous guilty verdict. Any more time and I would have had to include compulsory jury IQ testing in my petition to the Ministry of Justice too.

The judge sentenced him straight away. Nine years imprisonment.
The journey home on the last day of a long trial always feels like an anti-climax. Today is no different. As I sit down in an empty carriage, ready for one last long trek back to London, I begin to unwind, and as I watch the picturesque scenery rolling out silently outside, I feel a small sadness, a strange emptiness, a chapter has ended, all the busying around has stopped, the case is finished, and there is nothing, yet, to replace it.

Whenever I have a choice of taking a fast-expensive train which zooms through the countryside with a powerful shudder and arrives back in one of the main London terminals within a blink of an eye, or a slow cheap version via Clapham Junction, I take the latter. Not that I am a lover of railway travel, but it makes financial sense, and 'it all adds up' as my husband is fond of saying. Today I am facing twenty-one station stops. I know the route well; I have probably sat on that train at least fifty times over the last few years. Every now and again I amuse myself by trying to list the names of all the stations from memory, I don't think I ever succeeded, but I keep doing it. As I stare at another station sign, I try to imagine what it would be like to live here. Who lives at Martins Heron anyway, I never see anybody get on or off at Martins Heron. And why Martins Heron, what does that mean, was there a guy called Martin who had a heron? I must look it up. As the geographical distance between me and the trial increases, my mournful feeling of loss starts to fade. By the time we get to Staines the train is full, and I am beginning to look ahead, almost ready to leave the events of the last couple of weeks behind. I wonder who is going to be at home when I arrive.

Wednesday, so the girls have no clubs, they should be there. Today I am looking forward to listening to their daily dose of school dramas without the trial snatching part of my attention. Clapham Junction at last. I change trains, and it is still a couple more stops, and then a short drive until I open the front door, but Clapham Junction feels like home, I am back.

Later this evening, I am making myself chorizo in wine with pasta, red peppers, and feta. I pick up a frying pan from the cupboard and put it on the stove. I stare at it, pick it up again, bounce it in my hand, I feel its weight, note the thick curved steel, I admire its perfectly round shape. What force would I have to use to dent it as badly as Exhibit LBNX-01?

Gender Discrimination Within Criminal Justice System

If you are a woman, gender discrimination in the criminal justice system is something you learn to live with or you change industries and become a midwife.

I am not usually too fussed about equal rights, I do not mind having my shopping bags carried and doors opened for me, and being chauffeured around, but there are days when even I want to scream, come on, give us, women, some credit!

My client today is a woman in her early 30s, who has clearly invested time, effort and money to look her best possible self. I am particularly drawn to the eye-catching creation on her head. Her hair style is short and sharp, with vibrant pink and blue streaks on top. The number of charms on her Pandora bracelet says money is no object when it comes to looks and adornments. Her jacket is real leather, her handbag designer, her figure bikini ready, she looks the business and she makes me feel like a poor relative.

She is unmistakably Polish, so I introduce myself. We chat non-committedly about her level of English, the weather, our respective commutes to court. I notice with amusement that we are both being in fact very English in our small talk.

A few minutes later a scruffy looking overweight man comes up to me, perspiration control is clearly an issue for him, and he says dzień dobry, which means hello, good morning, I think you are going to be my interpreter too. His t-shirt is faded, his jeans stained, his hair greasy and his teeth, well, let's not go there. I look to the woman for an explanation and she says in a tired voice, he is my husband. We are separated, she adds promptly, wishing to vindicate herself.

They are jointly charged with conspiracy to facilitate entry to the UK to person or persons who were non-EU citizens, knowing or having reasonable cause for believing that the individuals were not citizens of the EU. In simple terms, people smuggling.

The conspiracy involved others too, I hasten to clarify for those of you conversant enough with the law to know that husband and wife cannot be charged with conspiracy involving just the two of them. The law protects couples from being accused of conspiring with each other. This has always intrigued me somewhat. Husband and wife can be jointly charged with murder, but not with conspiracy to murder, unless others conspirators were also involved, no matter how much conspiring the said husband and wife did in preparation of the substantive crime they eventually committed.

Back to my visually mismatched clients. I don't think they realise how serious the charge is yet, but this is about to change. The barrister arrives. I worked with her before, she is a no-nonsense down to earth woman who just likes to get on with it. We have a pre-court conference. I learn that the woman was caught red-handed, two Middle Eastern females were found concealed in her specially adapted car in Dover, pretty clear-cut case, she admitted it all to the immigration and police already, and is going to plead guilty today. She is visibly shaken when the barrister tells her that she is looking at 4, 5, possibly more years in prison, but she composes herself quickly.

The husband is pleading not guilty, as he claims he had no knowledge of his wife's actions, he had no idea she was involved in assisting anybody in entering the country. He had no idea that his vehicle, which he happened to be driving to France at the same time as his wife, but with his young son as a passenger, was similarly adapted, leaving a large space behind the retractable roof folding compartment. His wife bought both cars. He had no idea the cars had been adapted in any way, either before or after his wife purchased them. He has never heard of a Middle Eastern individual named Mr M, who entered into a business transaction with his wife, loaned her the cars, and promised financial reward for successful completion of her part of the deal. He had no idea why there were suddenly two cars parked outside their house, and why she told him that he was welcome to drive one of them on his trip to Poland, where, he says, he was going to have some dental work done, but alas, his son was taken ill not far into France so he had to turn back and was on his way back home in the UK when he was stopped by immigration, first in Calais and then detained in Dover. No illegal immigrants were found in his car.

The barrister leaves me alone with the defendants for a few minutes. The husband decides to use this opportunity to share his views on immigration with me. He says that as a Polish national and a patriot he finds it insulting to be on trial for facilitating illegal entry of non-EU citizens into the country, he tells me he is innocent because he does not like those immigrants, he is against allowing them to enter Britain, in fact, as a practising Christian, he doesn't tolerate them. It takes me a moment before this sinks in. I bet he will be among the first ones to demand ongoing 'rights' for EU nationals after Brexit. Rights to what? Rights to stand against everything Britain holds dear? Rights to ongoing racism? Where does the irony even begin?

The barrister is back and asks him, repeatedly, whether he still categorically maintains his innocence. He denies all knowledge, adamantly so. The barrister finally tells him with a sigh, that it is of course his choice, but the prosecutor would be more willing to get the wife off the case, despite her being caught with the actual females in her actual car, than believe his protestation of innocence. The crown prosecution believes, the barrister continues, that he is seen as a much more likely brain of the whole operation and the wife and children were just a cover up. Simply because you are a man, she adds, not too impressed with that train of thought herself.

We are called into the courtroom. First the arraignment, then trial preparation formalities, finally the judge addresses the husband and tells him to use the intervening months between now and his trial wisely because if he is indeed innocent then all well and good, but if he is in fact guilty and just hopes for the best then he has made a poor decision today. There can be little doubt what the judge thinks of the husband's lack of knowledge.

We leave the room and during post-court conference the husband sits quietly at the back, while the three of us, the barrister, the wife and I vent our displeasure with both the prosecutor, male, and the judge, male, for doubting the wife's ability to commit the crime all by herself, no matter how much pre-planning and level-headedness this might have required, without her husband's help or knowledge.

It is the 21st century for crying out loud, women are capable of committing a sophisticated crime without having to rely on their husbands, thank you very much!

On this note we say goodbye and it's off to the train station for me.

Today's hearing takes place in a picture-perfect historic town in Kent. These picture-perfect historic towns scattered all over the South East, are places of great beauty and are ideal for a weekend break, but on a damp cold Monday morning, as I rush to get there for 9.30, and then rush back out as soon as my timesheets are signed, to get home at a reasonable hour, local charms are lost on me. This afternoon, head down, umbrella to the wind, I average six miles per hour according to my fitness app. Its 20 minutes exactly solid march along city walls to the station, I know, I have done it before, and today I have 22 minutes to my train. If I miss this one, it's 45 minutes to the next one, and then its touch and go whether I catch a connection at Bromley South. I am pretty sure I would pass an 'advanced level trainspotting' exam with flying colours, especially on South Eastern, Southern, and Thameslink time tables. I am still a bit shaky on South Western Railways.

It takes me all the way to Sittingbourne to stop panting from that speed-walking exercise.

As I get comfortable with a Kitkat and a discarded Evening Standard in a fairly empty carriage, my thoughts return to the husband and wife in today's case. I try to imagine what the prosecutor and the judge in today's case would think of power dynamics in my own marriage.

Would they similarly insist that my husband must be the brain behind any plan of action, and the manager of any task we undertake together, simply because he is a he and I am a she?

Would they see me as a little wife, her indoors? Would they still think the same if they paid a visit to our home, true fly on the wall style, and tasted my husband's Sunday roast, at which he excels, and watched him sew buttons on school uniforms, and then saw me taking care of our children's passport renewal, filling in bank account applications, discussing garage conversion with our builder, sorting out money for it, coordinating holiday dates with other events, booking flights, hotels and car rental for the whole family, including flights for his mother to see her sister on another continent, organising our social diary, including dinners with my husband's friends, arranging theatre trips, and weekends away to picture-perfect historic towns?

I am a total control freak and I find it difficult to be truly happy unless things are done exactly the way I like them done. My husband treasures peace and quiet above everything else, and loves his sofa time more than life itself. He is also incredibly domesticated, he weeps with joy when new shoots from his strawberry bush take roots, and he puts flea spray on the cats, or whatever it is that you put on cats. He cooks, he bakes, he roasts, he bastes, he chops, and makes smoothies. He leaves taking care of family logistics and entertainment to me. What do you make of that, your honour?

A Week in The Life of a Trial

Day 1

This week British taxpayers' money is being spent on a two counts of rape trial. The complainant in the case is a girl who replied to an ad on a popular Polish website. The defendant is a Polish guy who, in his own words, felt a little lonely in his marriage and decided to look for elsewhere. Defence claim it's a sex for money arrangement turned sour, the prosecution say the woman got raped during a job interview for a secretarial position. Defence say the ad was in the 18+ Erotica section of the site, the complainant maintains she responded to a job advert in the General Jobs category. As far as discrepancies in evidence between parties go, this case is up there with the best of them.

The seriousness of the charge dictates that a rape can only be heard in a Crown Court. The seriousness of the charge also means that the atmosphere in the courtroom can be tense and unpleasant for everybody involved. A lot depends on the judge in the case, how they manage and diffuse a highly inflammable situation without trivialising the matter in any way.

Our trial is a 'floater', which means the first morning was spent waiting for a courtroom to be allocated to us. At 2.30pm we found a temporary home for the next week or so, unpacked all the props, we managed to swear the jury in and we listened to the prosecution's opening speech introducing the case.

The judge said the usual bit that judges always say at the beginning of a trial. He half turned towards the jury and spoke in calm, measured tones; "Ladies and gentlemen, we both have an important role to play in this trial, but our roles are very different. I am the judge of the law. This means that I tell you what the law is as it applies to this case and you must accept any legal directions from me. I will also remind you of some of the evidence at the end of the trial. However, you are the only judges of the facts and I cannot tell you what the facts are. If you feel that I have left out an important piece of evidence or give wrong emphasis to any piece of evidence, you give it the weight which you think it deserves."

I have heard this speech so many times, I am beginning to mouth the words with the judge halfway through. It feels like a meditation mantra, and it always has a reassuringly soothing effect on me.

Day 2

Just to give you an idea how well such trials, which have the potential to irreversibly destroy a person's life, are prepared.

The alleged crime occurred eighteen months ago.

Yesterday, when playing the victim's video-recorded interview, called ABE (achieving best evidence), to double check if it was fully admissible and could be played to the jury today, it became apparent at the 26th minute, out of total length of 75 minutes, that we were watching the wrong, unedited version of the recording.

The victim referred to events, which had previously been agreed between parties as either having no relevance to the case, or having the potential undesirable effect of unfairly influencing the jury regarding the complainant's bad character, which should have no bearing on the matter in hand.

The wigged and cloaked prosecutor and defence barristers then spent close to an hour manually editing the tape, which simply meant that they played it, stop and started it and wrote down minutes and seconds to skip when playing it to the jury. Needless to say, the rest of the playback was of somewhat reduced quality, the frequent stops and starts significantly detracting from its content. Another obviousness is that it should not be the barristers' job to edit evidential tapes in the middle of the trial. This should have been done months ago in a police forensic lab. The correctly edited tape apparently exists, it just never made it to the courtroom.

Another thing, minor or not, depends how you approach details of evidence in rape trials, is that the alleged victim claims she found the advert in the General Jobs category on a Polish job website and not, as the defendant maintains, in the 18+ Erotic category. This was explored at some length in cross-examination. Nobody however went on the website to check that in fact there is no 'General Jobs' category on the said website.

There is more. All independent witnesses need to be checked for relevant criminal convictions, and especially any history of perverting the course of justice or similar offences which might undermine their credibility as witnesses. One rather important defence witness's criminal record is being checked this week, the week of the trial. If the results from Poland are not obtained by Friday, he will not be allowed to give evidence.

My long morning commute is almost done. The next station is X, where I get off. I half-expect to hear the tannoy, *Alight here for potential miscarriages of justice, and administrative errors.*

Day 3.

Everybody begins to be drained by how slowly the trial progresses. Long running trials usually follow the same pattern, which all the long in the tooth professionals recognise and accept as standard, they might even find comfort in the familiarity of it all, but which might be confusing to newcomers to the system. Quite a few defendants are newcomers, just like my client this week, a first timer. I am usually quite proud of them, most of them are quick learners and by the end of first day of their trial they adjust to a court pace.

A typical court day runs in short spurts of frantic rush followed by long periods of frustrating inactivity. We seem to go from ushers literally jogging between courtrooms, witness rooms, photocopying rooms and CPS rooms, to forlornly staring at walls in eerie silences. Defendants, with the best will in the world, are not always able to fully understand all the reasons for delays. I am used to being asked regularly, 'so what exactly are we waiting for now?' Once a trial begins, barristers never seem to have enough time for proper conferences with their clients, their conversations rushed and disjointed. Defendants usually voice their frustration to me on day three. The only comment I can offer them is a rather lame experience-based wisdom, 'it is just the way the system often works'.

Day 4.

Today was dedicated almost entirely to advocates arguing with each other so aggressively that the judge had to tell them off in an exasperated head teacher's voice, Mr X, Mr Y, you are both professionals, you are both adults, please try to remind yourselves of these simple facts and act upon them. This type of in-trial squabbles goes by the fancy legal name of voir dire hearing.

The jury is always absent from the courtroom for the duration of any legal arguments that might arise during a trial. They are kept in the dark as to the reasons and content of any such arguments. What happens is, one of the barristers stands interrupting the flow of a witness's evidence, and says rather enigmatically, your honour, a matter of law has arisen. That is a cue for the judge to turn immediately to the jury and say, ladies and gentlemen, I must ask you to leave for a few minutes, my counsel wish to discuss a matter of law with me.

Today a few minutes lasted several hours including the lunch break. I can only imagine that it must be frustrating for the jury to be asked to leave the room for no apparent reason and then to be kept in the jury waiting room for hours, only to be told on their return to the courtroom, ladies and gentlemen, I apologise, this has taken a little longer than anticipated but we are now in the position to continue. No clues about what was being discussed while they were out.

Legal arguments usually tackle admissibility of evidence, disputes over line of questioning adopted by the counsel for the other side, answers given by witnesses, and how it might unduly influence the jury, and lead to ambiguity and speculation, and how to limit the damage just done and prevent any further slippages of a similar kind. The majority of 'matter of law' discussions occur whenever a witness strays into a minefield of irrelevant, hearsay, or prejudicial material and the opposing party feels the need to redirect the examination back into evidentially familiar territory.

Day 5.

We are actually making good progress today. The wheels seem well oiled and our chariot of justice staggers ahead towards half time, when prosecution rests and defence team take over. Police interviews are being read out, of which there were three in total. A few matters of law arise again. This is not uncommon in cases where the defendant's first language is not English. Issues surrounding availability and quality of interpretation during interviews are being explored, no irregularities found. The jury learn about detention logs, custody records, and police codes of practice, division of labour between arresting officer, investigating officer, custody sergeant and police station cleaner thrown in for good measure. The judge is visibly pleased with his flock today, he actually congratulates both counsels for the lack of sniping in the courtroom. It's Friday all around, and we finish at a decent time, 4.30pm.

The trial will continue well into next week, the defendant being less than half way through his evidence, but my account ends here. I will now let you move on with your lives, whilst I watch whether the life of at least one protagonist in my trial changes for ever.

On second thought, it is probably not fair to leave you hanging here, so I will tell you that after two weeks' trial the defendant was acquitted of both counts of rape and the complainant was branded an opportunistic liar, so it took a long time, but we got there in the end.

Knife Crime

Knife crime is treated extremely seriously in this country. Some areas of Britain are so badly affected that hardly a month goes by without yet another young man being stabbed to death, or at least it feels that way. Bearing that in mind, my own professional experience of knife crime is limited and thankfully marginal. Two names come to mind, Daniel and Mariusz.

Daniel was in his mid-twenties when I interpreted for him during his two day Crown Court trial for 'possession, in a public place, without a reasonable excuse, of an article which has a blade or is sharply pointed, where the cutting edge or its blade exceeds three inches, or 7.62cm, contrary to section 139 of Criminal Justice Act 1988'.

On a warm summer night, Daniel was enjoying a barbecue with friends in a park in North London, when a group of young orthodox Jewish men were passing by. Daniel asked one of the men for a cigarette. The man ignored him and walked on. Daniel did not like that response and spat in the direction of the man, shouting angrily after him, words that the man later claimed amounted to racially and religiously aggravated abuse. Police were called and dutifully arrested Daniel on suspicion of the above. Whilst searching Daniel's backpack an officer found a small kitchen knife. Daniel was charged with racially aggravated common assault and possession of a knife.

In order not to prejudice the jury against the defendant, as it was never suggested that the knife played any role in the incident, each charge was dealt with separately. The jury acquitted Daniel of the assault charge at another trial some months earlier, so the second trial dealt solely with the possession of knife in public place. Daniel's defence always was that he had had the knife with him that night to cut Polish sausages for the barbecue. A sample Polish sausage was duly presented at court by Daniel's defence team to demonstrate to the jury that it was indeed the type of sausage that would require a sharp knife to cut it. Two police officers gave evidence, Daniel was cross-examined at length about Polish barbecuing traditions, and his feelings about members of different faiths, his girlfriend gave tearful heart-felt evidence in his defence, and we listened to impassioned closing speeches. The jury took just over half an hour to acquit Daniel of the knife offence.

As he was leaving the dock, Daniel punched the air hard with his fist. Months of legal nightmare over, he could move on. He wasn't particularly bitter, just happy to finally get his life back.

Mariusz was in his late forties when I met him at his first hearing at Magistrates Court. Mariusz faced the same possession of knife charge as Daniel, in his case it was a folding knife found at the bottom of his backpack, under a pile of personal possessions.

It became clear from a short conversation with Mariusz that he attracted bad luck wherever he went. Six months before he broke his leg whilst jogging. The fracture was so bad that he required two surgeries, and a metal rod was inserted in his thigh, he still limped visibly when I met him.

A few days before his arrest his niece asked him if he could help her with a school project, which involved making a boat from a material of her choice. Mariusz agreed to help, and they went to the park together and found a piece of half-burned wood that Mariusz planned to carve the boat out of. He brought the knife with him to clean the wood initially. He then continued carving the boat at home, his niece added a few finishing touches. Mariusz's boat won the competition, and was on display at the school for several weeks.

A few days later, a nice afternoon in early September, Mariusz went for a slow walk in the park, he was still on crutches. While there he noticed two of his acquaintances, a man and a woman, both Polish, having a heated argument. He came closer and asked the woman if she was all right, as the man was getting more and more aggressive. A few minutes' later police arrived. It turned out that an anonymous passer-by had called the police, concerned for the woman's safety. Since both men were Polish, speaking almost no English, the police assumed they were both involved in harassing the woman, and all three people were taken to the police station. Mariusz was initially arrested for intimidating behaviour towards the woman, which was later confirmed to be groundless, but on his arrest his backpack was searched and the knife was found. Mariusz had forgotten all about the knife, but it was still sitting there, in his bag, since the day he started carving the boat for his niece.

At court he pleaded guilty to the possession of knife, and he received a sentence of a community service, consisting of 150 hours of unpaid work. He also had to pay £85 prosecution costs, and £85 victim surcharge. He gasped when the sentence was read out.

Mariusz was not particularly bitter, after all he respected the laws of his adopted country, and he just saw this experience as another stroke of his typical bad luck. He was looking forward to the time when he completes the unpaid work and gets his life back.

Daniel and Mariusz's cases are both examples of a knee-jerk reaction to the real problem, a mere footnote in the country's knife crime story and I only hope never to find myself involved any deeper into it than that.

My First Time

They say you never forget your first time. They are right. My adventure with court interpreting started one warm June morning, on a 6.45 from Streatham Common to a Far Away destination, change at Clapham Junction. I arrived at Far Away Crown Court with my stomach in my throat or my heart in my stomach, I was not sure which at that point.

Court number four first floor. Up a wide staircase and here I was. Six defendants, four men, two women, all Polish, all in their mid to late twenties, all jointly charged with affray, and two more interpreters.

I missed a fast train connection at Basingstoke and so was the last one to arrive. The two other interpreters looked totally in charge and on top of things. My first instinct was to say sorry, I don't speak English, or Polish, whichever would have got me out of there quicker.

I did not follow that instinct and minutes later I was allocated a pair of my very first clients by one of the other interpreters.

The other interpreters were both local and when I said cheerfully that I had just travelled from London, they scrutinised me for other signs of insanity.

"How long did it take you to get here?"

"Three hours."

"And how long will it take you to get back...?"

Phew, they were suddenly much less scary. I can do this.

We went in, and I remember not being able to hear much at all, the judge was softly spoken, we were huddled up in the dock together, all nine of us behind a thick glass wall, plus a couple of guards jangling their heavy key chains every now and again. I despaired and I panicked. Months of preparations, hundreds of pounds spent on gaining top industry qualifications, and here I am not able to interpret anything because I cannot hear a thing. Two minutes later a hand of one of the other interpreters shot up. Second phew of the day, they couldn't hear either. We got a pair of headphones each. Everything was now loud and clear, every single word. Beautiful!

'You are charged on this indictment that you were involved in an affray involving five others...' I beamed ecstatically at my client as I interpreted my first ever sentence in a court of law. He threw me a dirty sideways look, second time within the last hour somebody questioned my sanity. It took me another half an hour before I managed to wipe the excited grin off my face.

The trial lasted nearly three weeks. The commute was a killer, three hours door to door each way, six hours every day for three weeks, I must have been crazy. I was an exhausted wreck at the end of it, but a very confident, pleased with herself wreck too.

Any trial that runs into weeks rather than days runs out of steam eventually, because, I mean, there is a limit to how many independent witness accounts of the same drunken incident involving broken flower pots and urinating in public anyone can listen to before the story loses its momentum. In the case of my first trial, thirty-two people were called to give evidence. The entire street, the whole neighbourhood got to say what they remembered of that night when a group of heavily intoxicated Polish immigrants set off to destroy their front gardens.

The case involved a group of friends who decided to celebrate Easter by getting together for a hard-core drinking session on the beach, and then on the way home, late at night, as they walked along a quiet pebble-stoned street, one of them felt like spicing things up a bit by kicking a terracotta flower pot and smashing it to smithereens. Their behaviour provoked an irate reaction from one resident who ran into the road and urged them to get a move on and fast.

This rebuke did not go down well with my clients. The resident was a mixed-race man and so one of the Poles decided to tell him to go back to his effing country. This caused the resident to hit the roof, as he was not only British born and bred, but he was also a soldier, recently returned from a mission in Iraq. Being told on his own doorstep, by a drunken Pole of all people, to go back to his country was high up on his zero tolerance responses and he might have overreacted somewhat. Things escalated from there, but, luckily in the circumstances, nobody suffered any serious injuries and the sum total of damage caused were a few irreparably broken plants pots and a badly traumatised old lady from number nine.

The Iraqi war veteran's father, a true British gent, took it upon himself to strengthen the prosecution case with his own thorough scientific research. He prepared pages and pages of diagrams depicting terracotta plant pots of varying sizes, complete with calculations of impact they would have had and the severity of potential injuries inflicted, should any of such plant pots be lifted and smashed on a hypothetical victim's head. Complete with vectors and equations in italics, this was proper A-level physics material.

Some facts from this trial have faded slightly over the years, but these few details still stand out, because they are true gems and they are hard to outshine in the, you-could-not-make-it-up sort of way.

Or perhaps it's just that people really never forget their first time.

The jury found all male defendant guilty as charged, both women were acquitted. After the verdict the case was adjourned for sentencing hearing, which I did not attend, and I never found out what sentences they got.

My Big Fat Trial

Not all clients I work with are ethnic Poles. Some of them are Polish Roma travellers, more commonly referred to as Gypsies by everybody who deals with them, bar the most politically correct court officials.

In the majority of cases when client is a Polish Roma, I do not feel the need to divulge this information when I write about them, as it has no bearing on the story itself. In the case of theft, burglary or domestic assault it makes no difference.

There is however one distinct type of case which is commonly associated with Eastern European Roma travellers. I am not entirely sure how I should proceed with this subject not to cause offence, because facts, based on court cases and conviction rates are pretty damning, and the pattern of behaviour is unmistakable, and it points out to the fact that that Roma travellers engage in a modern slavery type of exploitation much more often than any other group of Eastern European immigrants to the UK.

These cases usually make the front page of the Daily Mail ... twice. First, the paper copies and pastes the prosecution opening speech delivered on the first day of trial, and for the second time after the inevitable guilty verdict by the jury.

Whenever a paper quotes the prosecution's opening speech in its entirety, it often has the effect of fooling the reader into thinking that defendants described in it have already been convicted of the offences they are charged with. The prosecution's approach is very clear. Everybody is guilty until, sometimes, the jury gets it wrong and acquits them. It is only the 'Trial continues' note at the end of such reports that indicates that in fact no verdict has been passed yet. However, this helps to sell newspapers. Daily Mail is currently (data as of June 2018) the UK's second largest newspaper by circulation, with The Sun topping the list. There is less than 200,000 between them, everything to play for.

Details of everyday lives of Roma travellers are almost completely impenetrable to outsiders. They keep themselves to themselves, they often lead their entire existence within the safety of their immediate family clans.

Traditionally, as a very minimum, the immediate family consists of three generations of grandparents, several children, and grandchildren living either all under one roof or in close proximity to one another. Roma marry and start having children extremely young, well below UK legal age, to which they have little regard.

I am yet to meet a 40-year-old Roma who is not a grandparent. Family is the centre of their universe, family ties are sacred to them, and they tend to focus all their energies and thoughts on family life. They have the luxury of doing so, because gainful employment, on the other hand, is not very high on their list of priorities. Various myths circulate about the list of professions that their culture and tradition allow them to undertake, and that list is not particularly long. Traditionally, one of the activities they are happy to engage in has been trade. They keep vague about other jobs that Roma code of conduct finds acceptable.

Roma Gypsies have lived in certain parts of Poland for several hundred years. Despite this long co-existence, nobody in Poland knows much for sure about Roma beliefs and customs because they do not open up about their culture, traditions and common law to others. In fact, they go to great lengths to keep their lives as obscure to the outside world as possible. Apparently, allegedly, a special Roma code of behaviour exists, which defines all their dos and don'ts in every area of life, but it is practically impossible to a non-Roma to access that code, so we, the outsiders only know it as rumour. In my experience of dealing with them, and fair enough, I only ever deal with Roma who have fallen foul of the law, they are always full of distrust towards strangers, always firmly on their guard, a layer of hostility barely hidden just beneath the surface of social interaction. They have their reasons. A lot of unhappy history lies between ethnic Poles and Roma Gypsies. Poland is not a country that welcomes non-Poles of any description with enthusiasm, and Gypsies are not a nation willing to integrate, as they believe that integration would bring about a destruction of their strong cultural identity. This is an unfortunate starting point to a relationship between ethnic Poles and Roma Gypsies and the relationship is marred by mutual suspicion and animosity.

In popular Polish thinking, Gypsies have a reputation as obnoxious petty thieves, dishonest con artists whose moral code allows them to steal freely from non-Gypsies. They are seen as a group of people who do not value education, are work-shy, lazy by nature, and unwilling to integrate. In fact, the word *Cygan*, which is the Polish word for Gypsy, is also one of the words that can be used as an informal synonym for the word thief. And the verb *cyganić*, derived directly from Cygan (Gypsy) means to lie, cheat, con, or swindle. This word is well established in the Polish language, and still commonly used, and so it is not unusual to hear, in Polish, are you trying to *cyganić* me? Meaning, are you trying to con me? Not exactly conducive to building bridges.

The situation is not being helped by the fact that Roma have their own Romani language which they use whenever they speak among themselves, and which serves as an effective barrier between them and outside world. Romani language is a fluid linguistic construct, it has many dialects, and it borrows heavily from the language of the host country where the Roma group settles. When I listen to Polish Gypsies speak their dialect of Romani, it sounds nothing like any language I am familiar with. It is also interspersed with a Polish word every now and again.

The only aspect of Gypsy culture that ethnic Poles not only love but are happy to embrace as their own, is traditional Gypsy music. Gypsy songs, with its dreamy nostalgic undertones, accompanied by the strumming of guitars and folksy accordion tunes resonate well with Poles, who see it as a reflection of their own Slavic soul, and no Pole worth their salt ever tires in their quest for their innermost soul.

It is against this turbulent background that I arrive at my local Crown Court for a trial of a seven-strong Polish Roma family. The weight of mutual prejudices sits heavily on my shoulders, decades of distrust stretch between us as I say my friendly dzień dobry to the group of them. It is going to be a long few weeks ahead.

When I arrive at court, I do not know details of the case in advance. Normally, I ask my client at least what the charges are. Today I do not ask anything. I cannot predict their reaction; I do not want to risk putting a foot wrong this early into the trial. They might offer effusive explanation, all talking at once, mixing basic facts with protestations of innocence and ululation about injustice of the system that accuses them of wrongdoing. Then again, they might say next to nothing and look me up and down with a suspicious glint in their eyes instead.

Finally, one of them starts a conversation, and before long I am able to work out that they are jointly charged with exploitation and modern slavery against three ethnic Poles. They say they only ever wanted to help out their alleged victims, and this is how they are being repaid for the goodness of their hearts. I nod my head slowly as I listen, as non-committal as can be.

Now I know what the charges are, I am getting a pretty good idea what this is likely to be about.

The practice that leads to the enslavement of Polish victims by Roma Gypsies in the UK always follows more or less the same route, the main features of each offence of this type are always almost identical, down to smallest details. It goes like this.

A desperately poor, often homeless Polish man in his mid-30s or 40s sits on a park bench in a small town in Poland drinking cheap cider. He has been sitting there for several hours for the last few months, because he has nothing better to do, nowhere to go. Locals avoid eye contact with him in case he asks them for money and pass him by without a word.

Then one day, unbelievably, it looks like his luck is about to turn when a friendly Roma man sits at the other end of the bench and befriends the Polish man. He comes across as understanding and compassionate, he is a good listener, and after a short while he has a proposition for the Pole, let's call him Krzysztof. He suggests that Krzysztof should leave his bench, his park, his town, and come to England, there is so much work in England, there is enough work for everybody in England, easy work too, and it pays well, you can buy a pair of shoes with one day's wages in England.

Krzysztof does not believe every single word the Gypsy says, I mean he knows that bit about shoes must be nonsense, but it still sounds amazing. The Gypsy has it all planned already. He will pay for Krzysztof's plane ticket, and he will put him up with his family. Krzysztof will not need to worry about repaying him for the ticket until he has been working for a few weeks, and then the Gypsy will just deduct the price of the ticket from Krzysztof's wages. He will also have to deduct some money for food and accommodation, because you know, everything costs money, even in England. They both laugh heartily at the joke. Krzysztof is moved to tears when he thanks the friendly Gypsy for his kindness. The Gypsy says, uncomfortably, people should help one another, they shake hands.

A week later, because, why wait, he has wasted enough time already, Krzysztof arrives at Stansted airport, the Gypsy's cousin picks him up and drives him somewhere for a couple of hours, in awkward silence. It gets dark, Krzysztof does not know a single word in English, the place names on the signs mean nothing to him, and he has no idea where he is actually being taken to. When he arrives to his new home, he is taken to a smallest room he has ever seen, but hey, there is a mattress on the floor and a chair for his clothes, what else does he need? A Gypsy woman calls him to dinner. Hot and steamy delicious homemade stew, lots of it.

The next day Krzysztof is taken by yet another Gypsy to a bank, then to an office of sorts, and there are lots of forms to fill in. Krzysztof does not even try to understand what he signs, it is all in English anyway. The Gypsy helps him with the forms, half way through the day he suggests that Krzysztof should give him his passport for safekeeping, he would not want to lose his one and only ID document, would he. Krzysztof happily agrees. He cannot remember last time anybody fussed over him so much, not since his mother died that's for sure.

The day after that Krzysztof is woken up at 5am and it's off to work. He is driven to a warehouse, where he is shown the ropes. The job is simple enough, sorting and packing vegetables, 10 hours a day, 5 days a week. Krzysztof wants to pinch himself; he still cannot believe his luck. This is more than he could ever wish for. He remembers how people in his home town used to say, never trust a Gypsy. What did they know?

Friday is payday and Krzysztof is quite excited about that, but one of the Gypsies tells him that he will not get any money this week, because you know, remember, you owe us for the flight and you know, the room and the food, it all costs money. If Krzysztof is a little disappointed, he does not show it. He was looking forward to holding British bank notes for the first time in his life today, but he will just have to wait a bit longer, not a big deal. The following week he is given a note. One twenty-pound note. He finds it too awkward to ask why so little, so he does not. Weeks and months pass. Krzysztof works hard, earns little and life no longer feels so great. The food is less generously offered, his room is cold, and the Gypsies get really angry with him every time he asks them for his passport back.

What Krzysztof doesn't know is that the Gypsies need his passport to open bank accounts and to make claims to various government benefits in his name. Krzysztof has no access to his bank account, he does not know how to check his balance, he is not aware of any benefits he might be entitled to, he's never heard of tax credit.

When physical abuse starts, he puts up with it for a while, but finally runs away and walks into a police station in the nearby town. He is interviewed by the police for hours, and is taken into a safe house as a temporary solution. He is treated with dignity and respect he never thought he deserved. He is seen by a doctor, a dentist, he gets help opening a new bank account, he is even given a small weekly allowance to cover his basic needs. He is awaiting the Home Office decision whether he will be considered to be the victim of modern slavery and a further decision whether he will be granted a discretionary leave to remain in the country, but for now he is surrounded by all the helpful support workers and house mates who have been through similar experiences. Every now and again the police contact him to obtain further statements to help them progress their investigation. Months, sometimes years later, the case is ready to go to court.

The above story is pure guesswork, put together after years of working with both the victims and the perpetrators of exploitation, but it turns out I am not far off and the current case follows more or less the same pattern.

The first two weeks of the trial are spent listening to the victims retell every detail of the exploitation and abuse they suffered over several months. There are three victims in total. A middle-aged man and a young married couple. It is a lot to take, the evidence does not flow, but rather is given in stop and start mode and we take frequent breaks. I feel drained and empty at the end of each day. One piece of evidence stands out. The middle-aged man, our Krzysztof from earlier on, is talking about being regularly laughed at and forced to behave in a degrading manner for the amusement of his oppressors. The prosecutor, clearly playing devil's advocate, suggests to him that surely, it was all good fun and he was probably enjoying himself at those Gypsy family gatherings as much as everybody else.

To which Krzysztof launches into an impassioned tirade delivered seemingly on one breath, there is no stopping him. "Excuse me, Mr Prosecutor, but which part of my nightly ordeal sounds like fun to you, is it the evening when they are all drunk and make a circle of empty beer bottles in the middle of the room and tell me to stand in the middle of the circle on one leg like a stork and they put a harmonica on top of my head and they make me sing song after song after song, and if I stop or hesitate they pour water over my head and then they make me play the harmonica but the sound does not come out because it is all wet from the water they just poured on me, or is it the evening when they send me to the bottom of the garden with a box of matches for light and tell me to search for potatoes they hid in the bushes for me to find and if I don't find them fast enough they punch me in the stomach and give me dry toast for dinner for the rest of the week as a way of teaching me never to waste potatoes ever again?". Krzysztof stops. The prosecutor waits a couple of minutes before his next question, making sure that silence sinks in and becomes more powerful than anything Krzysztof could have adduced to his evidence.

The jury arrives at unanimous guilty verdicts to all charges fairly quickly. Sentencing hearing follows and all seven receive immediate custodial sentences of varying length.

Sandra, the Roma family matriarch is stunned, unable to speak, her daughter in law's three young children face being taken into care.

The idea of having her whole family sent to prison overwhelms her. She looks straight past me when I say goodbye. The men in the family give up any attempt of controlling their anger any longer and I see a glimpse of that foul temper the victims described in their evidence. Their language turns vile too as they vent their frustration at being sent to prison for several years. Their deep distrust of me, which I pretended I didn't notice during previous weeks, becomes a thinly veiled resentment. One of them hisses towards me, 'I bet you are happy now!'. I am very grateful for the security guards pouring into the dock.

Walking back home on the last day of this case I go over a few details. Modern slavery is very different from traditional understanding of the term. I struggle to get my head around the fact that even though one of the 'slaves' was allowed to travel to Poland during their ordeal, taking her children with her, she chose to return to her 'masters'. This makes me think that at least some of the victims were at least partly willing participants in this practice. That is not to say that they were happy with the treatment received from the Gypsies, the financial exploitation, the physical abuse. There can be no excuse for what they were being subjected to. It does make me think however, that appalling and demeaning as their life with the Gypsies was, it was still better, still preferable to the life in Poland that the friendly park bench Gypsy pulled them out of. Otherwise, why on earth did they return to their oppressors? In the UK, with the Gypsies, they had a roof over their heads, they had hot meals the Gypsy women cooked for them every day and they had pocket money for cigarettes and sweets for the kids.

Back in Poland, there is no exploitation, no slavery. There is also no house, no work, no hot dinners.

The park bench is still there. Tempting.

Justice Without Borders

Extradition of Damian

When you hear the word *extradition*, a few high-profile cases might spring to mind. Annie Dewani's South African husband, an autistic hacker with a penchant for breaking into top secret Pentagon computers, and a few religious extremists being the most typical.

An average day in the life of Westminster Magistrates Court, the central extradition court in the land, is less newsworthy. Eastern European small-time would-be gangsters dominate the proceedings. An awful lot of new cases are being produced in court daily. So many in fact, that the court requires the full-time services of two Polish, one Romanian and one Lithuanian interpreter every day, including Saturdays and bank holidays. It has also recently started delegating some of the final hearings in the proceedings to another court in London.

Legal basis for extradition within the European Union is the European Arrest Warrant (EAW) issued by any EU member state. With relatively few exceptions, where the requested person is a heavyweight career criminal and proud of it, the majority of EAWs tell stories of broken childhoods, misspent youth, and sad errors of judgement, often buried in distant past.

A typical extradition case might go like this. A man in his mid-thirties, let's call him Damian, who has lived in the UK as a law-abiding citizen for several years, gets arrested at his home address in the early hours. He is not completely surprised by this, he knew in his heart of hearts that this was always a possibility, a fear he has learnt to live with but which has never gone away completely.

Extradition rule book stipulates that a person arrested on the EAW must be presented in front of the appropriate judge as soon as practicable. Each requested person is entitled to free legal representation by a duty solicitor at their first court appearance. Duty solicitor, more often than not accompanied by an interpreter, goes to the cells to have an initial chat with our Damian, to tease out all the important bits of information which will let him decide whether this might be one of very few cases where there is a chance of discharging the warrant. That initial lawyer-Damian consultation can be a real slog. Damian is often in genuine shock, as he watches his new life, he so painstakingly built in the UK unravel minute by minute. He is also often tired after a sleepless night at a police station. Not an ideal setting in which to focus on life changing matters.

Duty solicitors at Westminster deal with several extradition cases per day and it can be tricky not to fall into a rut and to still see each new case as a living person in a seriously bad place, rather than another lot of paperwork to be processed.

We begin conference.

- Were you aware of the proceedings against you in Poland?

- No, not at all. I thought it all ended a long time ago.

- A court in Poland imposed a sentence of two years imprisonment for your offences. The sentence was suspended for 5 years. Were you aware that the sentence had been activated?

- No, absolutely not, I had no idea.

- What were the conditions of the suspension of your sentence?

- I had to pay compensation and stay in touch with probation.

- And did you?

- Yes, of course.

- Did you inform your probation officer that you were moving to England?

- Yes, of course. I spoke to them about it and they were happy for me to go.

- Did you inform your probation officer of your new address in the UK?

- No, I didn't.

- Did you inform the court or the police of your new address in the UK?

- No, I didn't.

This exchange is subsequently repeated during each stage of the proceedings, with the defence barrister, prosecutor and judge asking the questions.

Based on answers to these questions, Damian is likely to be deemed a fugitive from the requesting state's justice system, as the truthfulness of his evidence is being challenged.

Defences against extradition available to Damian are few and extremely unlikely to succeed.

Still, defence lawyers put forward a mix of well-worn arguments, often knowing full well they are going to fail. Damian instructs his solicitors that he wishes to oppose extradition and to drag out the proceedings as long as possible. If he is released on bail for the duration of the case, he wants to carry on working to make provisions for his family before he is sent back. If he is refused bail, he wants to serve as much of his sentence in a UK prison, rather than a Polish one. There seems to be a consensus that Wandsworth prison, where vast majority of extradition candidates await their fate, is a highly preferable place to be receiving their punishment than any penitentiary in their home country.

The near exhaustive list of arguments against extradition is as follows:

Passage of time between the offences being committed and the EAW being issued, proportionality of the extradition to the seriousness of the offences in conjunction with passage of time and Damian's conduct in the intervening years. All of this leads us to the most commonly used argument, based on Damian's and Damian's family members' right to private and family life, referred to in short as article 8, as it is based on Article 8 of Human Rights Convention.

Contrary to urban myths doing rounds in the media which claim that having a cat is usually enough to successfully oppose extradition, it is in fact almost impossible to discharge the warrant based on Article 8 rights alone. It is not enough to have a family, young children and elderly parents.

For Damian to have even a remote chance of winning his case based on his right to private life, he would need to present the court with some seriously miserable circumstances of the said private life. He would need to be, for example, the sole carer for his severely disabled wife or child. The Article 8 threshold is set so high by rulings by judges in previous extradition hearings, that most cases are foregone conclusions the moment the judge formally opens the proceedings.

Bearing in mind the difficulty in opposing extradition successfully, why is it that most people in Damian's position still put up a desperate fight against it?

Let's have a closer look at Damian.

When he was 18, he got mixed up with the bad crowd. To impress his new friends, he vandalised his old school building. He kicked in a few doors and broke a couple of windows. He then proceeded to be rather rude to police officers who arrested him. He got suspended sentence for criminal damage and insulting a police officer. A year later he bumped into a friend who was in town visiting family on a short break from England. The friend told him that employment agencies in England were always looking for new staff. The work was hard, the pay was crap, but it was miles better than doing nothing here in Poland. Within a couple of months Damian was in Preston, working twelve-hour shifts in a warehouse, living in a shared house with seven other Polish workers just like him. That was 13 years ago. Today Damian is married with two young children, the family rents a 2-bedroom house, Damian works as a team leader for a logistics company, and his wife is a part-time cleaner at a local school. Damian has no criminal record in the UK. His children were born here, England is the only home they know. If Damian gets extradited to serve the 2 years sentence in Poland, this carefully assembled life will disappear.

The stakes are incredibly high and so Damian puts all his hope in the *passage of time-proportionality-article eight* combination which, his barrister informed him, might just tip the balance in his favour during his final extradition hearing in a few weeks' time.

Over the last few years I met quite a few Damians. This is understandable, as Poland is an unquestionable champion of the EAWs. Based on data available for years 2009-2013 Poland was issuing around 800 European arrest warrants every year. By comparison, France was issuing between 10 and 25 warrants over the same period of times and Germany around 30 a year.

To be completely fair here, for every Damian there is a Wojtek or two.

Wojtek comes across as a distinctly unpleasant individual for whom crime is a lifelong commitment and the only lifestyle choice he understands. He too, started young and by the time Damian got his fork lift driving licence in the North of England, Wojtek was serving a five-year sentence for robbery and GBH in Central London. His extradition case could not proceed until he completed serving his domestic UK sentence. He is wanted in Poland for a number of similarly serious offences. He has no community ties, no employment history to speak of and several recent convictions. At the initial hearing Wojtek protests his innocence and is adamant that the arrest warrant is one big misunderstanding. The judge refuses bail.

At this point I should be able to add that the choice of names is purely coincidental. Except it isn't. You see, Wojtek is the name of my first half-serious boyfriend, half because whilst I was totally serious about him, he was not serious about me at all, which he proved by brutally dumping me at the end of A-levels, my summer plans shattered.

I cannot shake off the feeling that the 'justice' of me continuing to exact petty revenge on Wojtek, my high school love interest, decades later, is somewhat akin to the justice of extraditing all the Damians to Poland for the sins of their youth.

The reality is that in most cases extradition is ordered by the Westminster court.

The requested person then has the right to appeal the extradition order to the High Court within seven calendar days, or to be more precise, the right to apply for leave to appeal. Provided they are granted the right to appeal, they appeal is lodged and the appeal hearing is listed at the Royal Courts of Justice within another few weeks.

It happens that by the time appeal hearing day arrives, and by the time the appellant sees the high court judge and barristers, looking magnificent in their robes and wigs from another era, his fighting spirit abandons him. At the beginning of the hearing, the judge addresses the requested person with all the formality the occasion requires, 'Mr Kowalski, we have come here today to hear your appeal against extradition ordered issued on …, by his honour District Judge…. sitting at Westminster Magistrates Court. The extradition order was issued according to section 5 of Extradition Act, 2003. We have given you leave to appeal the order and we are now ready to listen to any representations you might have in relation to this matter.

I interpret the judge's words, and am in turn the only person present in this beautifully furnished courtroom to understand the appellant's response, as he speaks in Polish. He says this, no less, 'Listen, whatever, fuck it, tell the judge thank you for coming, but fuck it, I do not wish to appeal any more, I am going back to Poland, fuck this'.

This potentially awkward situation is tactfully saved by the interpreter who makes a split-second decision that accuracy of translation will serve no purpose in this instant. I proceed thus, 'My lord, I do not wish to pursue my appeal against extradition any further, and I wish to be returned to Poland'. Wojtek, will be travelling on the Biggin Hill to Warsaw flight within ten days.

No Longer Welcome

Extradition and deportation originate from two very different sets of circumstances but since both potentially lead to the same end result, which is the removal of an individual from the country, these two terms are often confused, not least by the very individuals at the centre of the proceedings.

Put simply, extradition proceedings are initiated when a foreign country requests the return of an individual to that country, for the purpose of commencement of criminal proceedings against them, or to serve an already imposed prison sentence. Deportation is the expulsion of an individual from the UK because the Home Office rules that the individual is no longer allowed to stay in this country.

My experience of dealing with deportation is naturally limited to Polish nationals, which means I have knowledge of a small fraction of numbers and issues involved in the subject. One observation that I became aware of in the last year or so is that although a certain number of Eastern Europeans have been subject to removal from the UK every year since eight (so called A8 (Accession Eight)) countries from the region joined the EU in 2004, there has been a noticeable increase in the rate of EU deportations as well as the acceleration of the removal process since the Brexit vote.

Everything I describe here relates to EU nationals only, I am aware that significantly different rules apply to similar non-EU cases.

Broadly speaking the Home Office has the right to initiate deportation proceedings against an EU national in one of two scenarios, with a degree of overlap between them.

Firstly, UK Immigration authorities have the right to deem an immigrant undesirable and request their removal from the country based on the individual's persistent criminality, both in their home country and the UK.

Not exercising 'Treaty Rights' is the second basis on which deportation of an EU national can be sought. This phrase is the official speak shorthand to describe immigrants, frequently homeless, who do not work and do not access the benefits system to support themselves in this country. The Home Office says it is in public interest to have them removed.

When dealing with Home Office detainees, two literary quotes come to mind, 'that which does not kill us, makes us stronger' and 'Abandon all hope, ye who enter here'. By the time detainees manage to access interpreting services, they would have endured a couple of long, frustrating days when nobody was able to give them any specific information in relation to grounds of their detention, the appeal process and deadlines, or timescales of anything. Accessing legal advice also seems an impossibility at times.

Standing next to a person appealing a deportation order, their sense of desperation is particularly strong.

A typical Polish deportation candidate is a profoundly lonely man, usually middle-aged, afflicted by addictions, he speaks virtually no English, and has very little understanding of how British healthcare or welfare systems work, and therefore had not been able to access any help and support successfully when there was still time. He is not even aware what help and support are potentially available. Remember Krzysztof, a Pole forced to play harmonica for the Gypsies? He is one of them. After jumping over the fence in the middle of the night, and escaping the Gypsies, Krzysztof was found walking along a motorway, confused and exhausted. Hours of detailed interviews with the police and later on with the Salvation Army, he was placed at a safe house, and enjoyed the 45 days allowed by the Home Office for 'recovery and reflection' after an initial decision was made and while the National Referral Mechanism (NRM) was deliberating his longer-term fate. The 45 days is a magic number given to everybody in Krzysztof's circumstances and these six and a half weeks are often, sadly, the most dignified and luxurious period in these persons' lives. Krzysztof received a small amount of spending money every week, he was seen by a doctor, a dentist, he had a new bank account set up for him, and had his own room with a bed in it. He was never hungry, nobody shouted at him, nobody made him do any chores beyond keeping his room tidy.

Unfortunately, Krzysztof's lifelong demons did not wait long until they returned to haunt him. A long-term alcoholic, he went back to heavy drinking within days of being placed in the safe house, and within hours of receiving his first weekly allowance. Against strict house rules, he kept alcohol under his bed, got drunk most days and every night. He got verbal warning, written warning, final warning, and eventually was asked to leave. With no money, no job, no language, no friends or family, he walked to the nearest town, where he became street homeless, he got together with other homeless Poles, and stole food, stole alcohol, stole wallets and handbags, tried his hand at burglary, got caught, tried again, got caught again, court cases followed, fines remained unpaid, community orders were breached, prison sentences short at first became longer each time. Krzysztof was given several last chances but having blown them all, he did not have much fighting spirit left when Immigration finally caught up with him a couple years later. A few weeks ago I saw him for the last time. His puffed-up face red and sweaty, his moustache unkempt, his movements slow, his thinking muddled. The appeal hearing did not take very long, and he never stood a chance. He spoke so softly, I could hardly hear him, but what he said had heart-breaking poignancy. He would like to be allowed to stay in the UK because he had nothing to go back to in Poland. He would like to stay because his life was so much better here than in Poland, and he had prospects and hope for better future. The Tribunal judge treated him with utmost dignity and respect throughout. Three weeks later Krzysztof received a letter notifying him that he had lost his appeal against deportation order and he was sent back to Poland shortly afterwards.

His story had gone the full circle. In a few months' time he would start questioning whether his English adventure wasn't all just a drunken dream, too surreal to have actually happened to anybody.

High-handed Hague Justice

Most of the time when court interpreters meet, we swap stories of recent cases, trying to find a lighter side to the world of justice, to make it all sound a little more approachable, entertaining even, less formal, less gruesome. There is however one category of cases that is no laughing matter whichever way you look at them, and as a rule we don't really like to talk about them that much. These are Hague Convention child abduction cases. Everybody always loses in this type of cases, even though they might not always see it that way on the day.

These matters always follow the same formula. A single parent, usually the mother, leaves the country, in this case Poland, with a child or children, without asking the child's other parent for consent. Typically, they travel to the UK from a small-town best known for high unemployment, high rates of alcoholism and petty crime. In Poland, mother and daughter, let's call the girl Julia, shared a sofa in the living room in a rundown house rented by Julia's grandmother from the local council. Other inhabitants in a mould-ridden property included Julia's grandparents, aunt and uncle and their three children. Julia's mother turned up on the doorstep when her relationship with Julia's father disintegrated amidst alcohol-fuelled domestic violence and death threats. Julia, now 7 years old, last saw her dad four years before when he turned up, drunk, at Christmas, asking Julia's mother for money.

When a good friend emailed Julia's mother from Yorkshire saying how absolutely fantastic life was up there, and why don't they come over, it should be easy enough to find cleaning or factory work, and they can all share a flat, at least to start with, she did not need much time to think about it. It was matter of weeks before mother and daughter were peeling their eyes for the white cliffs on board the Pride of Dover. After initial few weeks they rented a small but clean flat, Julia had her own room for the first time in her life. She started school and made new friends. Mother worked two jobs, as a cleaner and a kitchen assistant. She met other Polish mothers at a local Polish shop. There is at least one in every town in England these days. Mother and daughter were truly happy. They bought a hamster, and called it Kubuś. Julia was really good at maths and sport. She struggled with English to start with but was catching up fast, teachers were pleased with her progress. The mother dared to dream about content and happy years ahead for both of them.

Then one day, five or six months into their new exciting life, police knocked on their door. The mother was handed a court summons for the child abduction case to be heard at the Royal Courts of Justice in London. Their travel documents were seized.

What had happened was, Julia's father made an application to the Central Judicial Authority in his country, requesting the summary return of his child to the country of her habitual residence, Poland in this case. His application was based on the provisions of Hague Convention in relation to child abduction.

From then on events unfolded rather quickly. Hague convention cases are treated with expediency and efficiency that might be sometimes, ...erm, less evident in other courts.

The aim is to get the judge to rule in this type of cases within six weeks of the UK receiving a request from a foreign court.

Mother met with the solicitors, who told her that there exist very few defences to Hague Convention cases that could be mounted, and the majority of cases end up with the court inevitably ordering the summary return of the child to the country of origin as the UK is obliged to honour their international obligations imposed by the membership of the Convention. CAFCASS (The Children and Family Court Advisory and Support Service) officer got involved and they interviewed Julia, asking her whether she objected to going back to Poland. Julia was 7 years old and did not understand fully, if at all, what objecting to something meant. She said that she did not want to go back to Poland, she liked it here in England, and she had made lots of new friends. CAFCASS officer wrote a detailed report to the court based on the interview.

During final hearing in the abduction cases the judge makes it usually very clear from the start that unless the mother is able to provide evidence of exceptional hardship the child would suffer on their return to Poland, the return will be ordered. The barrister addresses the judge, and on mother's desperate instructions talks about how much better the child's life is in the UK, how they would be going back to sleeping on sofas and relying on handouts, and lastly, how heart-breaking it would be for Julia to be parted from her hamster.

Judges usually do not even need time to gather their thoughts while preparing their judgements in these cases, as the majority of Polish cases are clear-cut and the judgement is a formality.

Kubuś the hamster might get a mention in the judge's speech, only to say that the separation from a beloved pet cannot be treated as a serious enough obstacle preventing the UK from fulfilling their international obligations set out in the convention.

Mother and daughter were on the Ryanair flight to Poland within a couple of weeks. After another month or so, their life in England was beginning to feel like it had never happened.

When the news of their return reached Julia's father, he stared into his pint and gloated. He had showed that bitch who's the boss.

Forced Adoptions. When life punches hard

Polish immigrants in the UK typically list separate hot and cold-water taps, carpets in the bathroom and fake friendliness as the most annoying cultural differences between the two countries. Sadly, a growing number of Polish families live to experience a much more life-changing difference, in the shape of dramatically different approach to social services interventions in family life and, what sometimes sadly follows, forced adoptions.

Adoptions of Polish immigrant children have been a sensitive and heart wrenching subject for several years now. I have first-hand experience of many such cases, and to say that it is frustrating doesn't even begin to describe the issue. I have interpreted in more adoptions hearings than I would ever wish to get involved in.

Adoption, or 'placement' applications as they are formally called, are lodged with family courts by Local Authority's Children Services division, commonly known as social services.

Social services involvement in family life is something that my clients wouldn't wish on their worst enemies. The fear of social services, or SS as they are frequently called in the community, is paralysing among immigrant families. Polish language media in the UK regularly publish alarmist articles, 'SS target Polish children!', 'Polish children snatched by SS'. Obvious historical references are lost on no-one.

The articles make uncomfortable reading. They lay bare the fact that there is very little understanding of the role and responsibilities of child protection services among Polish immigrant population in the UK. Differences in the approach are immense between the two countries in this area. This subject is so complex, and emotionally charged that I find writing about it in an ordered way particularly challenging.

The parents involved often see their children as the only good thing that has ever happened to them in their otherwise miserable lives. Lives marred by physical abuse, poverty, drugs, alcohol, depression, and a raft of other mistakes and misfortunes. They see the children as the only certainty, the only hope. They know they are not ideal parents, but these are their children, how can somebody possibly take them away from them. And for what?

"Are you seriously telling me that just because my husband hits me every now and again, my children can't stay with me?"

"Yes, I have smacked them on occasion, they need to learn to listen, and they need to understand discipline. I was disciplined by my father, and so were my brothers, there is nothing wrong with it."

Add countless variations on the theme, and you will begin to get the picture.

Parents go through months, sometimes, unbelievably, years of proceedings, which involve care plans, child protection conferences, numerous court hearings, interim care orders, parental assessments, viability assessments, contact centre reports, CAFCASS (Children and Family Court Advisory and Support Service) reports, and interviews with independent social workers, psychologists, psychiatrists, support workers.

All this can be totally overwhelming for the parents. Frequently, they lack intellectual, mental and emotional capacity to understand and cope with all the stages of the process. Often, too, they are suspicious of the system and are reluctant to engage with professionals.

With very few exceptions, they love their children very much. And the children love them back with all their hearts. I know this, because the mothers in particular tell me how much they love their children every morning, every lunchtime, during every break. I also know this because all the lawyers involved in adoption cases tell the court this several times during each day of a five day final hearing, at the end of which the most likely outcome will be long term foster placement in case of older children and adoption in case of children under five years of age. Unfortunately, love seems not to be enough for these parents and children to stay together.

This is where parents really struggle to comprehend the process, this is where their clear uncomplicated logic fails them, the logic that says we love them, they are part of us, nobody will love them the same way, how can taking them away from us be possibly better for them than staying with us?

They also say, that in Poland, apparently, and just for the record I have no easy way of verifying this claim, so I just repeat here what they tell me, time and time again, that in Poland they would be allowed to keep the children and nobody would be interfering with their family life, as long as the children are loved, and the parents have a roof over their heads.

Forced adoptions is one of those subjects where I am glad my role at court does not extend to making the final decision in the case. My role as the person from whom the mother hears that decision first is hard enough.

End of An Era

Rumour has it that the going rate for a fully managed Polish wife is £14k. 'Girl only' option is cheaper but it covers introduction only, and then you are on your own, responsible for completing all the paperwork, setting up a convincing marital home and preparing for a possible Home Office inspection. And if you are really strapped for cash, you can always take a chance online, but then you will have only yourself to blame if it all goes belly up.

When I first started working for the Immigration Tribunal it truly felt like stepping into Narnia.

A quick glance is usually enough to work out which marriages are genuine and which are a business transaction. A good indication is a scenario where husband and wife can hardly communicate. The wife doesn't speak a word of Punjabi, Urdu, Tamil as the case might be, and the husband knows just enough swearwords in Polish to get by in Ealing Broadway. Both speak badly broken English. In the waiting room they behave like strangers, the only relationship that ever existed between them is that of a client and a service provider. Today he is a dissatisfied client, not happy with the service received.

Dialogues between my clients, usually the wives of appellants, who had been denied their leave to remain applications based on suspicions that their marriage was not genuine, and the Home Office lawyers who interrogate them, are cringe worthy. You have to be there to believe them.

- So, do you speak Hindi, Mrs X?

- No, I don't

- Do you speak Polish Mr X?

- Not well, but I get by

- Ok, please say something in Polish, the interpreter will assist us.

- Dziękuję, nazywam się X, jestem 38 lat, mój żona jest piękna.

- I dutifully translate this as 'Thank you, my name is X, me 38 years, mine wife beautiful'

- Have you got a religion, Mrs Y?

- Yes, I am a Catholic

- And does your husband have a religion?

- Yes, he does.

- What is his religion, please?

- I think it is, you know, oh, what is it called, I think it is Muslim, muslimic religion. He believes in Muslim.

- Mrs Y, would it surprise you to learn that your husband is actually a

Hindu?

- Oh, ok, maybe, I don't really know all the religions in his country, sorry, this is not something we talk about.

- Let's try an easier question. What colour are the curtains in your bedroom? Husband says blue, wife says we do not have curtains in the bedrooms, we have wooden blinds.

You get the idea.

Working on this type of cases used to be just plain uncomfortable, the day was punctuated by awkward silences and a lot of looking down to avoid the judge's eye.

Recently, with Brexit hard on our heels there is a strong feeling that time is running out, so attending these hearings has taken on a nostalgic undertone, like waving goodbye to a soon to be bygone era. With the rights of the EU citizens facing uncertain future in the UK, becoming an EU wife might be a dying trade.

On the way home I have a look at my own marriage. I had my doubts before marrying my husband. He came from a different hemisphere after all. He grew up dividing the year into two seasons, winter and summer. Nobody told him about spring and autumn, never mind about the Indian Summer, bless him. Several decades later, he still struggles to understand that April is not summer, and the start of bbq season is still far off.

His idea of a perfect snack is a stick of desiccated meat of dubious provenance. As a child he used to spend Christmas Day by the pool and Christmas dinner was a piece of barbecued steak and beef sausages with corn pap, except he didn't even know how to call it properly, so he called it mielepap. He had mango and avocado trees growing in his garden.

Mangoes in Poland of my youth came twice a year from Cuba, I tasted my first avocado at the age of 23 when I moved to London and I was not sure whether it was safe to eat it raw.

I wonder how we would fare if Home Office launched an investigation into credibility of our marriage, or our sanity of going through with it. Would my husband pass the test based on colour of the carpets or dates of birth of our children or would they send him packing? Good job he didn't marry me for a visa.

Stepping Out of the Dock

Interpreting in the Community

Despite best efforts by criminally active Polish immigrants in the UK, there simply aren't enough court hearings nationwide on any given day to provide full time work for all Polish court interpreters out there. To make ends meet when crime is slow, we are forced to leave the reassuringly grandiose confines of the Crown Courts, and accept other types of work. This is what happened to me last summer when I did.

It started with a buzz of a text message in my pocket. A text usually means, mummy please make sure you top up my parent pay account before lunch, but it can also mean a last minute, as-soon-as-you-can-get-there urgent and exciting job offer, so I checked it straight away. It was a job for the following morning, local authorities' job, not court, so commonly seen as second best by nearly all interpreters who know their worth, actually, cross out 'nearly', by all interpreters who know their worth. The post code caught my eye though, where do I know this post code from, it looked strangely familiar, teasing me to remember it, and then I clicked, my children's primary school! My youngest daughter completed primary education six years ago. I celebrated with a really good wine and an atavistic dance, no more school runs ever, ever, no more no more ever again. I was so ready to close that door firmly behind me, reclaim my mornings, and never look back. Funny thing, time, six years later now and the familiar post code made me all fuzzy. That school played a big part in my life for fifteen years, casting a shadowy presence over our family dinner table. That post code kept my children safe, dry and happy for approximately 270 weeks each. They learnt an awful lot at that school, some of that education will stay with them for the rest of their lives. Let's just say that by the time the text message buzzed, the passage of time had made memories of the school fond enough for me to accept the job for old times' sake.

Whenever I accept a local authorities' job, I do not know the exact nature of the assignment until it unfolds. On this occasion I was not sure whether it was going to be a straightforward parent-teacher consultation to discuss their child's progress, or whether it was perhaps an emergency multi-agency meeting called in response to a serious incident.

The next morning, I arrived at the school nice and early, and was shown to one of the eerily silent, empty classrooms. As I waited for others to arrive, I studied the walls carefully, in the irrational hope that I would spot a baby face of one of my children somewhere, but six years is a long time in the life of a local primary. A few minutes later the head teacher arrived, followed by two other members of staff, all of them breaking into a surprised smile of recognition as soon as they saw me. Seeing them all again was odd, and I do not have a rational explanation for this, but instantly unnerving. As soon as they all greeted me with their carefully measured smiles, not too cold, not too warm, just right, all the school rules and regulations, all the principles and procedures I used to scream inwardly against so many times in the past came rushing back to me. Too late to run now, I had to see this meeting through. It will teach me not to get sentimental about post codes. I still had no idea what the meeting was to be about but I could see it was something serious, with all the senior staff members in attendance. People always assume that interpreters would have been briefed about details of the case they are requested to assist with. Interpreters are not briefed, not ever. You have heard it here straight from the horse's mouth, so now you know.

The social worker arrived fashionably late and flustered, did not smile, did not apologise for her lateness, sat down and went straight to the point. Everybody in the room, except me knew why we were there, I resigned myself to trying to work it out piece by piece from what was being said. I worked out by then that my client was the mother of a couple of children from the school, who had still not arrived. I identified myself to the social worker as the mother's interpreter, she barely acknowledged me, and addressed the audience somewhat chaotically, 'yeah, all right, I'd be surprised if the mother turns up today, but let's give her a few more minutes, let me fill you in on latest developments in her absence, interpreter, please stay for the time being'. There was not much for me to do but sit back and listen. As the social worker began telling the story, adding names, places and circumstances, I got an uneasy feeling that I might know the family, not very well, but enough to feel uncomfortable, their story was beginning to sound more and more familiar. By the time the social worker, let's call her Laura, mentioned the oldest child by name, I was certain. That oldest child went to the same class as one of my daughters for seven years. My daughter had no time for boys, she thought they were all morons, but there could be no mistake, he was definitely one of the boys in her class whose name she used to mention when she wanted to demonstrate how stupid the male of our species are. From what I can remember that boy sat right in the middle of my daughter's moronic scale, she considered him no more or less of a waste of space than any other boy.

Whenever such circumstances arise, an interpreter is expected to exclude themselves from the proceedings quoting conflict of interest. Knowing your client socially or even casually within the community, is seen as a potential risk to impartiality, a foundation stone of public service interpreting. I raised my hand as soon as Max's name removed all doubts about the family's identity, but Laura frowned at the interruption and gestured me to wait, she was on a roll, filling everybody in the room with details of a rather unpleasant incident that took place at the children's family home on the weekend. Increasingly uncomfortable, I waited, and continued to listen, aware now that the head teacher and others must have also realised that the family was too well known to me and I should probably not be working on this case.

As soon as Laura finished her presentation, I said what I needed to say. A short, unpleasant exchange followed, 'why did you accept the job in the first place if you knew the family?', 'I wasn't given any details beforehand, the only name on my job sheet was yours', 'Well, you should have mentioned something earlier', 'I tried'. 'What's done is done, please could somebody escort the interpreter from the room'. 'I can find my own way out, thank you, I know the school well', I said goodbye to all the teachers, one by one, addressing them by name, I could not resist that, and left the room. When I got home, I got a rather nasty email from my agency informing me that social worker Laura had complained about the interpreter not alerting her to the clear conflict of interest until half way through the meeting. A couple of eloquently composed emails later, the agency and I resolved the issue, all was good. After all, my client never showed up, so no harm done. I was excluded from working with the family, which suited me perfectly, I did not wish to come face to face with Laura again.

In some parallel universe where public service interpreting works perfectly well, this would have been the end of my involvement with this family. As it was, it took two weeks until I felt another buzz in my pocket. Two hours, as-soon-as-you-can-get-there, at a supervised contact session at a nearby contact centre. The text was followed by a phone call, could I possibly go there, it is really urgent, blah blah, blah. I find it difficult to say no on the phone, and the moment the agency can hear hesitation in my voice they know they have just got themselves an interpreter, so I say, ok, fine, I'll go, kicking myself as I say it. Not only has my working day just got two hours longer, but interpreting at a supervised contact is not the most pleasant or experience, but then again somebody has to do it or kids do not get to see a parent that day.

Supervised contact sessions take place at a contact centre, a parent usually has one or two hours with their children, in the presence of a supervisor who makes notes how well the contact is going. The notes are then sent off to the social worker in the case, and later analysed, and reported on during next family court hearing. In families where parents do not speak English and communicate with the children in their own language during contact, an interpreter is required to interpret parent-child conversations to the supervisor. As I said, it is not pleasant. I feel like a spy, a snitch, a rat, and I get dirty looks from children and parents alike every time I relate the content of their conversation to the supervisor. Not my favourite type of work, so I do not accept contact assignments very often if I can help it, but this time I got ambushed on the phone.

As soon as I saw the children's names on the contact list register, I realised this was the same 'conflict of interest' family I conscientiously excluded myself from interpreting for. That worked well, I sneered to myself, and decided that I was not going to deprive these kids of two hours with their mother, so I said nothing. If the agency are unable to put measures in place that would prevent me from being booked to work with this family, I am not going to insist on not working with them. I had not seen the children's mother for six years. The change in her was devastating. Physically she looked ravaged by, not sure what exactly, alcohol, drugs, illness? Mentally and emotionally she barely held it together, she was irritable, red-eyed and nervous, clearly somebody on the brink. I am not sure if she even recognised me. Max, her oldest son did, but pretended not to, the two younger boys had no idea I knew the family, they were toddlers last time I saw them at the school gates.

The contact went as well as it could in the highly artificial settings, which allow the family no privacy, where every word and every gesture is being recorded in the notes. The mother tried to recreate as much of their usual domesticity as was possible within these constraints. She brought home-made Polish food, which the boys ate hurriedly, making sure there was still enough time left for kicking the ball outside, a rushed chat about school and homework, and for a quick cuddle for the youngest two.

Watching parents' endeavours to squeeze a week of family life into a couple of hours supervised contact makes for pretty heart-wrenching viewing. Acute awareness that my presence diminishes the quality of the experience even further for them makes it barely manageable.

Saying goodbye was tender, tearful, and excruciatingly sad to watch. As I was leaving the room, I nodded goodbye to the mother. She gave me a look of utter despair and replied, 'goodbye, please try to come to my contact again'. Great, this was all I needed. Clearly, she not only recognised me, but she also must have seen me as some sort of reassurance amidst the collapse of her life, and would like me to return.

The mother, and I think it is high time I gave her a name. Magda sounds good, so Magda was on edge, distressed, confused and close to tears. During contact I remained impartial, relating accurately everything that one of the boys was hurling towards the mother, no matter how deliberately hurtful it was. 'First you left us, and now you pretend that you care again', 'I don't even want to come here anymore, you just cry all the time, you are no fun'. As I interpreted all that word for word, my sadness and concerns for the family deepened, all rules of professional detachment discarded.

A few weeks later Magda was evicted from the flat which she used to share with her three children for several years. The flat was basic, but she transformed it into a warm loving home for the boys, working all hours to keep their rooms filled with toys and books, and the fridge well stocked. With all three children in foster care now, Magda was no longer entitled to the benefits which had made the flat affordable. Magda used to work full time for various Polish companies around London, where English was not required, but after the children were taken away, her health, both mental and physical deteriorated badly, and she was no longer able to hold down a job. One way or another, and I do not know all the details, she came to the attention of local mental health services who found her a place in supported accommodation.

She moved from a three bedroom fully furnished family home where she cooked, washed, ironed and read bedtime stories to a single room in a hostel where it was just her and four badly wallpapered walls.

I could not begin to imagine how she was coping, it seemed to be the case of blow after blow, a sustained, relentless assault on her endurance. As it turned out she was not coping, and after a theatrically desperate suicide attempt, she was admitted to a local psychiatric hospital.

In the six months that passed since the 'conflict of interest' day at the school I had watched Magda rant, shout, scream, lash out, go silent, struggle, give up, try again, then finally deteriorate rapidly and collapse in defeat.

When I think of her now, I see a hounded animal, scared, shaking, hiding in a dark corner, and I do not care how clichéd that comparison sounds, it's the one that works best here. I look back to the time before it all went wrong, I remember Magda laughing out loud at the school gates, surrounded by her Polish friends, showing off a new baby in her arms. I even remember that same laughing out loud sound during an early contact session, when she was possibly still too shocked to grasp the seriousness of the situation. And then there must have come a moment when it all sank in and overwhelmed her.

The moment when she realised that no court in the land would return the children to her care in the foreseeable future, if ever, and that realisation overpowered her. Being a mother is all that matters to her, nothing makes sense if she cannot look after her boys. It is impossible to imagine her laughing out loud any time soon. The feeble smile she gave me at the contact centre haunted me on the bus home, and the next day and the day after. It haunts me still.

It has been a while since I last assisted Magda at the contact centre. Her children are still not sure why she hasn't turned up to several contacts in a row. The youngest one is not buying the foster carer's lame excuse that mum is not been feeling well, and instead sees her absence as clear proof that he was right all along and that she doesn't care about them after all.

A Day in the Life of a Telephone Interpreter

There comes a day in the life of every public service interpreter, when there are no court cases in our language within fifty miles radius, and no solicitors need to see their clients. That's when telephone interpreting comes in and saves us from daytime TV.

First call of the day comes as soon as I log in. Welsh police, executing a warrant based on Protection of Children Act, acting on information received that indecent images of children were being accessed at the address. Tense conversation, ending in inevitable arrest of the suspect.

A series of early morning GP appointments in quick succession follows. Workers, popping in to see a doctor on the way to work. Bad back, niggling cough, cracked skin on hands, indigestion, liver blood test results, problems sleeping, depression. An army of warehouse and factory men, pushing themselves too hard, too long, until finally their tired ageing bodies refuse to work with them.

Coarse voices of heavy drinkers, long-term smokers. They feel awkward, self-conscious, they see this appointment as a failure. Most GPs have got used to using telephone interpreters with their non-English speakers by now, because telephone interpreting has practically replaced face to face interpreting in almost all areas. Still, there are GPs, and patients, who are not happy with having the interpreter on the other end of a phone line and not in the room with them, and they make it very clear that this is not an ideal situation for them, and they would prefer a 'proper' interpreter. I stay calm, it's only 10.15am, I have a long day ahead of me.

A twenty minutes' lull follows, during which I check and check again whether I am still logged in, I do a phone line check by calling my landline from my mobile, I panic, what if I have no more calls today, am I becoming Jeremy Kyle prime audience? What if nobody needs an interpret.... the phone rings.

An older lady is at the police station, tearful, lonely, and upset, she's come to report a theft from her hostel room. I recognise her weak tired voice; I spoke to her a few times before. She feels that nobody listens, nobody wants to help. The police officer is asking my opinion, always tricky, whether I think there might be mental health issues at play. I reply that it is not my place to offer opinion, I am not qualified, this is not my role, besides, I cannot even see the lady, the officer quickly says, I know I know, it's just that we really do not know what to do with her, the officer also recognises my voice, she knows the three of us meet regularly over the phone. The client just wants to talk to somebody in her own language, so the conversation becomes chaotic, incoherent, the officer lets her talk to me for several minutes, I try to make notes, as much as the lady's rambling style allows, I look down at my piece of paper, a string of words, they do not add up to a story, but they do make a sad reading. After a while, without warning, the officer takes over the call again, and simply says, thank you interpreter, I think that's as much as we can do for her today, she is not interested in listening to what the lady has just told me, I begin to scribble over my notes even before we end the call. I think about this lady later in the day, I think about her sad lonely voice, I cannot picture her, but I can hear her very clearly, I feel cornered by her voice.

I take a break. Breaks at home are tricky, how long is not too long? I make coffee, check on my sleeping hedgehog, which annoys him, take out the washing, 15 minutes, I go back up.

I run a one woman two guvnors show most days, so now I take a call from another agency. These calls are mainly from the States, mainly from Illinois. I've been doing this for a while now, but the Chicago calls continue to feel unreal. Clients are old, born in 1930s and 1940s, sometimes even older. The oldest ones are usually in hospitals, recovering from major operations, they speak in feeble voices. Some calls are heart-breaking end of life discussions. The other day I spoke to a lady who told me, whilst we waited for a doctor to come into her room, that she was born in Wołyń (Volhynia), before the war, and that her mother was tortured and killed, she asked me if I heard of Wołyń, and she carried on talking about it. Everybody with links to Poland has heard of Wołyń, currently Western Ukraine, it was a place of widespread ethnic cleansing massacres against the Poles during Second World War. The name is synonymous with unimaginable horror and genocide atrocities. I cannot begin to imagine what horrors she must have gone through at a young age that it compels her to mention it 75 years later, to a complete stranger on the other end of a telephone line four thousand miles away.

Back to the UK. New patient GP consultation. The patient casually rolls off previously diagnosed peripherally calcified pineal gland cyst and requests a referral to neurologist.

This is when years of compulsive viewing of Holby City and Casualty pays off. No medical condition is too big or too small for me, linguistically speaking. Hypertrophic cardiomyopathy? Bring it on. Paroxysmal nocturnal haemoglobinuria aka PNH? Not a problem.

After that I spend an hour with a CBT patient. Mental health therapy sessions via telephone interpretation service might, at first glance, sound like a definition of madness, but it actually works well. For a non-English speaking patient, in order for them to access these services at all, an interpreter is a must anyway. When the interpreter is a voice on the other end of a phone, patients tend to relax more, the setup removes a layer of awkwardness they might feel with yet another person present in the room with them. I love interpreting during CBT and other therapy sessions, especially when it is clear that the client opens up and starts talking freely about their feelings. Trying to convey their emotionally charged messages accurately I really do interpret 'to the best of my skill and ability' as the interpreter oath taken during official face to face interpretation tells me to do.

Six o'clock. I log out. Tired, I go downstairs and make myself a cup of tea, I check on the sleeping hedgehog again, which annoys him, my head full of scraps of all the conversations I just had.

I might log in again later on. Chicago calls will be in full swing by then, with clients calling their health insurance companies, trying to make sense of the latest bill they just received. This is when I am most grateful for our National Health Service. UK evening calls are a selection of nervous mothers calling out-of-hours doctor's surgeries, and police responding to calls of domestic violence, or booking in drink drivers. I usually call it a day after a particularly obnoxious client in police custody decides to blame his current circumstances on me, the interpreter, and channels his anger into insulting me in the most flowery language he can come up with.

Telephone interpreting gives me second hand skills in multiple fields. I am a doctor, lawyer, public health nurse by proxy and I regale my family with my overheard medical knowledge regularly.

Hi, I am your Polish Interpreter, how may I help you?

Telephone interpreting is a proper mix bag experience, calls come in from both the UK and the US, and include medical appointments, prisons, detention centres, social services, police custody, safe houses, probation, victim support, NHS 111, numerous charities, energy suppliers, housing associations, 999 emergencies, as well as Viagra Savings Card activation line. Tone changes from call to call take some getting used to. As you can imagine, just looking at the list of clients, not every call is a barrel of laughs, in fact, most of them are not funny at all, so when a light relief moment comes, it is most welcome. Today, I had a few of those.

First off, came a call from a police custody suite, I was requested to assist with booking-in procedure of a newly detained person. These calls all follow a familiar routine and I could do them backwards, and without any help from a police officer at all.

- You were arrested on suspicion of assault and I have decided to keep you in custody as I have several objections to releasing you on bail. Firstly, there is a serious risk that you will not turn up for a court hearing, as you have no community ties, secondly you might commit further offences whilst on bail, and finally you might interfere with the witnesses in this case. Would you like to make any representations in the attempt to persuade me to release you on bail?

- Officer, I am the only breadwinner in my family, I have two children, one of them is a recently born baby, and if you lock me up I will not be able to support my family, and my wife and children will end up homeless, my wife cannot work because the baby is really small, and my son has been having serious health problems for the last couple of years and she needs to look after him, and he is always having hospital appointments, and GP appointments and blood tests, and I have to work really long hours to support the whole family and we have a cat too, and how can you say I have no community ties, my son goes to school, and I have a family here and I work as a builder, I have to keep working so my family have money for rent and food, and school clothes and otherwise they will lose the flat and my children will be taken into care.

- Sir, I am keeping you in custody for tonight until your court case tomorrow morning, I do not think your wife and children risk becoming homeless in the next 24 hours, do you?

Later this morning I was connected to an MRI scanning room.

During a patient pre-scan preparation, the MRI scanner technician decided he was going to learn enough Polish to be able to say to the patient, 'breathe in - breathe out' during the scan. After I spelled it out for him, he decided to do a dry run with the unsuspecting patient. I could hear him say to her, very pleased with himself, weeditch - weeditch, which is wdech - wydech (breath in - breathe out) in the original, but the subtle one sound difference in pronunciation was lost on him, and this rendered his best efforts meaningless. He did that before I had a chance to explain to the patient what he was doing. She was most amused and all anxiety she might have been experiencing up to that point, disappeared. All part of the service.

Telephone interpreting lacks personal touch, which is not always a bad thing, sometimes it puts clients at ease, they are more relaxed when working with a faceless voice at the other end of a phone line, so they are more likely to open up about their issues. This is helpful during mental health assessments and other similarly sensitive discussions. On the other end of possible scenarios, being an invisible presence in a room full of people can be frustrating especially when sometimes I am not even sure how many people there are. Clients do not always see the need to provide an interpreter with 'context', so I just do my best. Occasionally this leads to comic situations. The other day I had a long telephone interpreting session with two social workers on a needs assessment home visit. A face to face interpreter was booked, cancelled last minute, but they decided to go ahead with the visit anyway, as the whole family gathered for the occasion. Enter, me, through the loud speaker.

I was told that I would be interpreting for the mother of two underage children. Several minutes into the conversation I realised that an adult son was also present, but although he spoke fluent English, the social workers played it by the book, and the book says that family members should not be used as interpreters. The son and the two social workers all talked in English. None of them paused and asked me to interpret to the mother at any point, so I used a well-known interpreting technique called "butting in", whenever I spotted a convenient break in the conversation. This went on for a while, they all seemed happy enough with how the meeting was progressing. At some point, I butted in again, and delivered a long chunk of what had just been said. I was speaking for a good minute or so when one of the social workers said, interpreter, who are you talking to, the mother is not in the room right now, she went to the kitchen to make herself a cup of tea, we'll let you know when she is back. It is not often that I am lost for words, that would be unprofessional, but all I could do was open my mouth and close it again a couple of times.

I leave you with a selection of telephone interpreting exchanges which make my days a little bit brighter each time.

Booking in a detainee into custody at a London police station.

- Because you have been arrested, you have certain rights. You have the right to inform somebody of your detention. Do you want to inform anybody that you have been arrested?

- Yes, the president of Russia.

- Do you have the president of Russia's number on your phone?

- No.

- Then I am afraid we cannot contact him for you. Do you wish to speak to a solicitor, free of charge?

- No.

The female sergeant did not bat an eyelid, and delivered all of the above in the same monotonous police-speak.

***

- Hi interpreter, I am calling from a police station, I have a Polish gentleman here with me at the front desk, could you find out why he came to see us today?

- (Translated from original Polish, naturally). Sir, Mister policeman sir, I have nowhere to sleep, I came from Poland a couple of weeks ago, I was supposed to have a job, but it didn't work out, I have serious mental health issues, I mean I suffer from schizophrenia, and I would now like to go back to Poland but I have no money to go back. Oh, and I lost my passport, I think it must have slipped out of my pocket, so I have no document to prove who I am right now.

- Excellent, thank you, interpreter. A challenge, I like it.

***

- Police Officer: Interpreter, we have a lovely Polish lady with us, she is a little bit intoxicated

(I love police understatements), I'll pass you over to her, her first name is Królewna.

- Me: let me guess, her surname is Śnieżka?
- Yes, how did you know?

(Królewna Śnieżka is Polish for Snow White)

***

Telephone interpreting carries the inherent risk of descending into Chinese whispers style of comedy every now and again:

Speaking to Mr Shah, an orthopaedic consultant.

- Me: Am I on loud speaker?
- Mr Shah: Yes, you are allowed to speak...

And Another Thing

My position in the dock offers a unique perspective on what happens in the courtroom. Combined with propensity to form strong beliefs about everything that comes my way, this inevitably leads to my expressing highly opinionated views about various aspects of our justice system as I see it, from behind a thick layer of Perspex. Although I managed to smuggle a decent amount of ranting in previous chapters, I am far from satisfied, and now I am going to give myself free rein as I vent away.

Justice subject to Delays and Cancellations

Over the years I have learnt to accept that delays are an inevitable a feature of every trial. Unexpected twists and turns occur, witnesses notoriously say something totally new, something they never mentioned in their written statements, and when they slip it in for the first time from the witness box, before one of the lawyers manages to jump to their feet with 'your honour, a matter of law has arisen', the matter being that the witness had just revealed something he or she never felt worth mentioning until now, something which might potentially tip the evidence, and even if the judge directs the jury to ignore the witness's last answer, the jury cannot physically un-hear what they had just heard, so thoughts of discharging the jury and a re-trial are entertained for a while, until, usually, a decision is made to just get on with it anyway.

Other witnesses refuse to answer questions, or stubbornly reply they 'cannot remember' as an answer to every question, which amounts to the same thing. If they persist in their seeming lack of recollection of the events in question, this inevitably leads to another 'your honour, a matter of law has arisen' intervention from the barrister, and legal argument ensues on the subject of whether the witness has become a so-called hostile witness.

Discs with CCTV footage do not work on court equipment, jurors arrive late, and witness statements go missing. All this is to be expected and nobody involved in implementation of justice is surprised by a couple of hours of idle waiting time, and yet every now and again I am forced to ponder whether my capacity for being surprised might be insufficient for this job.

Yesterday I got up before six, chased my bus from the moment I saw it at the top of the road all the way to the bus stop, got to the station, punched the ticket machine fiercely, got a delayed train to Clapham Junction, sat for over an hour on another train, ran all the way to the courthouse door, but did manage to arrive on time for a pre-court conference with the client as agreed with his barrister. All this only to be told by the gaolers that the defendant was not on the prison van that had just arrived, and they did not have any explanation as to why that was at this point. All-righty then, I will have time for a coffee and a croissant after all.

At 10.00 we went into the courtroom whereby the slightly confused prosecutor had no choice but to inform the judge that the defendant was inexplicably missing from the court custody suite and requested more time to try and establish his whereabouts. An hour later we reassembled and learnt that the night before the prison van was delayed in traffic and when it finally reached the prison the gates were closed and the defendant was turned away. I could not help but imagine a medieval fortress with a drawbridge being pulled up at dusk to keep enemies away. The van driver then called a number of several local police stations until finally he found one with a spare cell for the night, two hours' away. The defendant was driven there and the van driver went home. This morning no transport was available to bring the defendant to court from nearly two counties away, but efforts were being made to resolve the issue as we spoke your honour, current ETA was midday. He finally arrived at the court building at 12.50. As courts break for lunch at one o'clock sharp, we adjourned until two. At two fifteen the judge called barristers only to his private room backstage. Half an hour later they emerged and the jury were called in for the first time in the day, only to be told that the judge's computer stopped working over lunch and since getting it fixed was likely to take a while, it was probably best to adjourn the case until the morning.

I braced myself for a two-hour journey home and walked slowly to the train station.

Your Honour, My Lord, Your Worship

At first sight some trials have everything going for them, but they just fail to pull it off. Sometimes, all the ingredients are there and yet, it does not quite gel.

At a recent trial, we had a truly Churchillian looking prosecutor, resplendid in his chubbiness, all pomp and circumstance and strawberry blond mop of hair. He pulled all stops and paraded his majestic persona with the greatest panache. He lost his cool frequently in the most glorious manner, punctuated by exasperated 'bollocks to that' whenever he tried to negotiate common grounds with his opponent. I suspect he appears disarmingly avuncular in his own family setting, but at court he was determined to be this formidable creature capable of stomping his exquisitely shod foot thunderously.

Pitched against him in Team Defence corner was a keen and eager, painfully intense, double-barrelled hipster-bearded youthful looking barrister.

The defendant was clean shaven, in a decent enough shirt and suit, somewhere between estate agent and a Tory backbencher, he looked like he hired a personal stylist to get it right for the occasion.

The interpreter had made an effort too, and she looked neatly professional.

We were all picture perfect.

I made myself comfortable in my seat. The view from the dock looked promising. All that was missing was a bowl of popcorn.

Enters the judge, centre stage. The judge was female and she was black, no doubt a woman of great importance. To have a woman trial judge is still somewhat more interesting than having a male one, for the woman to be black is just awesome.

And then it all began to unravel.

The judge decided to apply a strict schoolmistress management style to the trial. She was yet to grace us with a smile, and we were on day three. She had also decided to do away with anything that might be misconstrued as a sense of humour.

There was a woeful lack of chemistry between her and the young and eager defence counsel. In fact, they made a pretty convincing impression of two people who hated each other's guts.

This happens a lot in crown court trials, in fact, I can't remember a trial where the judge would not seem to be rooting strongly for the prosecution. The judges' leaning towards the prosecution side of things remains very much behind the scenes phenomenon, mostly invisible to the jury, I hasten to add. To be fair, judges do their level best to keep up their neutral guardian-of-the law impression throughout the official part of each day, only revealing any bias in the absence of the jury, whenever a point of law arises in the course of the proceedings and lawyers fight moot points of procedure between them.

Judges set the atmosphere in the courtroom.

The way the judge addresses the jury at the beginning of each trial is always telling about how the remainder of the case is likely to be conducted.

Jurors are always a big question mark, a dark horse in every trial. They are an impenetrable, 12-sided silent enigma, the bane of many a brilliant barrister.

Jurors are also, above all, not well versed in nuances of the law, that's the whole idea, to have twelve Tom, Dick and Harry's up there. For some of them, first day on the jury service is their first time ever inside a courtroom. The way a judge eases them into their responsibilities can make all the difference in how comfortably and confidently they approach their task. One of the first decisions a judge makes at the beginning of a trial is whether to go for a friendly ice-breaker and an encouraging smile with the jury, or whether to skip all niceties and dive straight into warning them of dire consequences jurors might face should they be foolish enough to research the case online in their spare time. Our awesome judge chose warning tone over friendliness.

Judges are largely responsible for how comfortable each person feels throughout the trial.

We all recognise that as long as we are in their courtroom, judges hold a degree of power over our lives, we respect their position, we bow in front of them in recognition of all they represent, and we retreat from the room walking backwards. I, for one, do not mind acting like a medieval serf during those moments, just to keep the show on the road, I signed up to this ritual of my own free will and eagerly so. We all did, with the obvious exception of the defendant drafted against his will.

Looking back, I remember this promising trial as one of the most stressful experiences in my interpreting career, with emotions running high and tempers flaring. Crown court trial by jury is by its very nature an onerous ordeal for the defendant, innocent until proven guilty. It is equally hard work for both barristers who are often pitched against impossibly arrogant opponents, against unexpected delays, and other bumps on the road to justice. The judge can make all the difference. They have a range of tools and attitudes at their disposal and what they choose to use in any given case has an impact on everybody. In this case the difference was between simply difficult and challenging and plain unpleasant.

Dear judges, as the Spidermen and Women, of the criminal justice system, so the fundamental rule applies, "with your great powers come great responsibilities".

As for myself, all I would ever ask for is the acknowledgement of my existence. 'Thank you, madam interpreter' at the end of the trial would make my day, and this chapter would not have been written.

Defending the Guilty

I used to wonder how defence barristers manage to do their job properly in some cases, purely from simple human decency point of view, it was the how do, they sleep at night type of question. And then I realised the answer was already there, in the very wording of the question. It's their job, and they want to be the best they can at it. Their career progression depends on the number and type of cases they take on. The bigger, the more seemingly non-winnable the case the better, so it's all to play for. Besides, somebody has to do it, in the name of fairness and in the interest of justice.

And yet. Some cases are truly morally repugnant and simply evil, they clearly have a victim and a perpetrator and frankly, the defendant's version of events is best described, and I am quoting here from a recent prosecution closing argument, 'fog and lies, ladies and gentlemen, fog and lies'. Still, every defendant who protests their innocence has the right to be represented by a barrister at their trial, the Rosemary Wests and Harold Shipman's of this world included.

During the trial, barristers seem to be fighting tooth and nail even on behalf of their least endearing clients, despite inevitably forming their own view of each client's innocence. They manage to stay polite and professional, and remain poker-faced with even the most deceitful, most obviously lying clients and this never ceases to amaze me.

I watched solicitors and barristers' skilful attempts to tease the truth out of defendants during the initial stages of trial preparation, when there was still time for them to change their plea and save us all a lot of time and embarrassment later on in the court. It was an ambitious goal, as a seasoned defendant's guard was always water-tight and it never went down.

A conference with a lying client is challenging to both parties. On one hand, the client must stay focused to make sure they do not say anything to incriminate themselves, which would make further representation by the lawyer untenable. The lawyer, on their part, must think carefully how to phrase questions in such a way that they are not likely to lead to an accidental admission of guilt.

Occasionally, defendant gets tired of this prolonged cat and mouse game and tries an 'honest' approach in their discussions with lawyers. To a depraved criminal mind confessing guilty truth to a lawyer who represents them is not in itself an issue. I remember a case where the defendant got exasperated by his own smoke and mirrors method of answering lawyer's questions, and finally offered, helpfully in his view, "why don't I just tell you the truth about what happened?". The truth that he might have had in mind sounded like a confession of guilt. The lawyer raised his hand, alarmed. Sometimes spelling out rules of engagement in big letters is the only way the lawyer is able to carry on working with a client. "If you admit your guilt to me, Mr X, I will no longer be able to represent you in this matter." This sounded like stating the obvious to me, but it elicited only a bored shrug from the client, 'I was only trying to help you do your job, I thought if you knew all the facts, you know, you would be able to prepare my defence better, you might think of something clever', he treated us to a rare sparingly-toothed smile.

Over the years I learnt that when you trade in justice, you follow the rules of your trade, just like any other. One of the rules, and it had taken me a while to get my head around this, is that truth plays a secondary role to the client's instructions. The moment it becomes clear that no amount of logic and reason will dissuade a defendant from pleading not-guilty, the truth had outlived its usefulness, and all efforts are mobilised to prepare as good a defence as circumstances and prosecution evidence allow. Once they take on a factually challenging case, a team of solicitors go over arrest statements, interview records and search logs with a fine comb, looking for an irregularity, technicality, anything.

A while ago I interpreted during a particularly nasty GBH section 18 trial, causing grievous bodily harm with intent, where there could be little doubt about the defendant's guilt. Stakes are always high at section 18 trials, as sentences on conviction are lengthy and run into several years. My client's barrister however, remained oddly confident throughout that his client would be unanimously acquitted by the jury. When I asked him about this, he explained that based on the totality of admissible evidence and a technicality relating to identification of the defendant by the victim, provided that the judge correctly applied the law to the case, an appropriately directed jury could not lawfully convict his client, and if they did, he would have grounds to appeal the conviction as he would argue that the law had not been applied correctly by the judge.

The truth did not get much of a look in. At the end of that trial, as I watched barristers pack up their belongings and exchange pleasantries with colleagues, I spotted it, the truth of the matter. There it was lying naked on the floor in the middle of the courtroom, in full view of anybody who cared to look, but we all scurried along, and left it there, discarded, soon to be forgotten. I didn't want it either, it was of no use to me. As an interpreter, my job is to render my client's 'truth' as accurately as I possibly can in English, and as long as I do that, I should be able to sleep at night. So why is it, that I am still thinking about this case and the many other similar cases long after they have been archived, why do I still see their faces and hear their voices.

Priceless Moments and Pet Frustrations

Barristers and Interpreters

What is it with barristers and their love of certain phrases? More personally frustrating, what is it with barristers doubting whether their interpreters are familiar with the said phrases? Third barrister in so many months asked me today if I knew how to translate the phrase an axe to grind. To be fair, crown court trials provide ample scope for that phrase to come to mind, and the axe, sadly, is not always metaphorical.

Later during the day, he asked me if I understood the phrase two-edged sword. I said I did, and I added, before I had time to bite my tongue, that my English really was quite good.

I do hope our relationship can still be salvaged after that because having the barrister and the interpreter who do not get on really does not help the proceedings.

Later still, we listened to the complainant in the case give evidence. She was also Polish, also assisted by an interpreter.

The complainant described the incident at the heart of the trial in following way; 'he said that first he was going to disembowel me and then he was going to chop me up in the bathtub' (Polish original, for those who know the language; 'powiedział, że najpierw mnie wypatroszy, a potem mnie posieka w wannie')

The CPS interpreter conveyed the above as, 'he said that first he was going to cut me into pieces and then he was going to cut me into pieces in the bathtub'.

The general idea was preserved, but it was not what the witness had said.

I am reluctant to criticise my colleagues' work. We all make mistakes, interpreting in the witness box can be stressful, especially for the first hundred times. Still, I was now more willing to forgive the barrister for doubting interpreters' professional abilities.

Don't get me wrong. Working with barristers can be a lot of fun. Whilst some barristers are regular enough human beings, reasonably grounded in reality, others go to great lengths to come across as eccentric masters of intellect and eloquence of deeply Dickensian provenance. They lug their larger than life persona with them at all times, and they come equipped with an assortment of props; archaic fountain pens, family crest signet rings, flamboyant cufflinks, monogrammed briefcases.

On the morning of the first day of a recent trial, the barrister took me aside and said that he would like to give me heads up that he would be using two idioms in his cross-examination of a witness and he was telling me this well in advance to make sure I would I be able to translate them into Polish when the time came. The idioms were 'an axe to grind' and 'keep things close to one's chest'. I reassured him that I would be able to translate them accurately. Over the next few days he took to tapping the side of his nose and saying 'remember, axe to grind and keep things close to one's chest', every time he saw me.

To my slight surprise, he did not use either of them in his cross-examination. When I pointed out the omission to him afterwards, he said, yes, well, I wasn't sure if they would translate well into another language after all.

On another occasion, in the pre-trial conference, a barrister tried to reassure the defendant that in his opinion, the opinion, which, between you and me and madam interpreter, he added, was shared by the prosecution barrister, the case was rubbish and should not have been allowed to progress all the way to a crown court trial. He then continued, as if having an internal debate with himself, that although the case was rubbish, the exact word he used was crap, let us not forget a famous English saying, madam interpreter, I hope you can find a good equivalent, pride comes before a fall. I remember, he went on, when in 1973....

As soon as this date was mentioned, I knew where we were going, we were going all the way back to Wembley, to that fateful 90 minutes, which cost England the World Cup qualification, and which saw Poland go through to the finals in West Germany the following year. The barrister then gave us a kick by kick, pass by pass account of the match, naming no less than six Polish footballers who took part. He told us he was actually there, as a wee lad, with his dad, level with the goal line. I contributed by reminding him, for completion sake, that Poland ended up finishing third in Germany, to which he replied, eloquently, in keeping with his barrister training, 'nah nah nah nah'.

The defendant we came to see in the cells was a lad in his mid-twenties and must have been ever so slightly taken aback by the fact that we were suddenly reminiscing about a football game from long before he was born, rather than discussing his imminent common assault trial, no matter how trivial the issue was in his lawyer's opinion.

Poetry in the cells

A sense of stepping into alternative reality hits me hard again today. My client is a smiling 19 year old charged with low level alcohol fuelled street robbery, criminal damage and two counts of spitting at the police officers which is formally, somewhat confusingly called assault by beating. He has no stable address and less than £5 to his name. At the end in-cell conference with duty solicitor he requests a pencil, but pen will do and some paper. Why, we both ask, puzzled. He would like to write a poem about his encounter with criminal justice system. I am dying to ask him if Oscar Wilde's Ballad of Reading Gaol was his inspiration. I stop myself.

Juries

Juries are a perfect example of, to borrow a classic line, a riddle, wrapped in a mystery, inside an enigma. During a trial we all glance at the 12 of them, trying and failing to second-guess what goes through their collective mind.

The jury sent the note to the judge today, 'do we have to be sure or is it enough if we are certain?'. I would love to be a fly on the wall to observe how they arrived at this question.

Slowness

The wheel of justice has only one setting, slow motion. Family courts add their own speed bumps to proceedings, despite their official mantra that reaching a solution expediently is essential in protecting children's best interests. More often than not, hearings are set several months apart, eliciting gasps of frustration from all emotionally involved parties.

Parents, whose children have been summarily removed from their care and who are determined to get them back, do not cope well with days, never mind months, of separation. In extreme scenarios my clients' exasperation rubs off on me. I am in the middle of one such case. The mother has mental health and addiction issues, she is doing her level best to deal with them. She was taken ill and was rushed into hospital unexpectedly on the day of previous hearing so the case was adjourned. Somehow, in the intervening months, the court lost sight of the reason for the adjournment and assumed that since the mother did not attend last time, she might be absent again this time, and did not book an interpreter for her. The case was therefore adjourned again, for nearly three months, due to court time constraints, with the clear direction to book an interpreter for the mother. That was a few days ago. The very prospect of having to wait 11 weeks before she is invited to give evidence about her progress in the battle against alcohol addiction seriously jeopardises her chances of winning that battle and what follows the favourable outcome at the end of the proceedings.

Unhappiness

I only ever deal with unhappy people. This thought struck me with acute clarity, as I was woken up at 5.30 this morning by a particularly noisy gathering of chirpily cheery flock of birds on my roof. It hit me and stopped me in my tracks. I am not sure how I feel about that. Does that leave me exposed, is my own happiness at risk? My mental health? No obvious answers presented themselves, so I carried on getting ready for another day with another unhappy client.

Frustrations

Frustration is an ever-present companion in my tireless efforts to assist in the so-called implementation of justice.

Frustration of spending an hour and a half travelling to the other side of London, passing 21 tube stops to a prison where the solicitors booked me for a legal visit and confirmed the visit with me by text, email and telephone a few days before. I have met the prisoner twice before and today's visit is just one of a series of conferences where we go over his confusing evidence and possible defence he claims he has. Progress is painstakingly slow, achieved on a weekly basis. I am quite looking forward to today's session, as it might be the make or break one, he might just understand that breaking one person's leg and another person's hand in two places cannot be seen as using reasonable force in response to perceived laughter at his expense because he was unable to make himself understood to a group of people at a bus stop whilst heavily intoxicated. He mistakenly assumed the people were Polish so he addressed them in Polish language.

I arrive with half an hour to spare, that's how I arrive everywhere, which means I am never late anywhere. It also means I spend even more time waiting for everything than is already included in the legal interpreter's job description.

Legal visits take place between 2 and 4pm. In this particular penitentiary it takes between 15 and 30 minutes to go through various stages of security checking. First, there is a solemnly celebrated task of finding the prisoner's name on the list, then comes fingerprint identification for regular offenders, I mean visitors. The fingerprint scanner can be temperamental, which can cause security guards to work themselves up into a state, which in turn delays the ceremony further.

Today, however, I do not even get to experience the doubtful pleasures of rolling my finger up and down the scanner. The solicitors have not turned up. They forgot to tell me that they had to cancel today's visit due to unforseen blah blah blah. Today's frustration might just top this week's list.

Frustrations are many. Frustration of spending an hour and a half travelling to the other side of London, passing 16 tube stops to a prison where the solicitors booked me for a legal visit and confirmed the visit with you by text, email and telephone a few days before. I have met the prisoner twice before and today's visit is just one of a series of conferences where we go over the evidence and possible defence he claims he has, slowly, painstakingly, on a weekly basis. I am quite looking forward to today's session, as it might be the make or break one, he might just understand that breaking one person's leg and another person's hand in two places cannot be seen as using reasonable force in response to perceived laughter at his expense because he was unable to make himself understood to a group of people at a bus stop.

I arrive with half an hour to spare, that's how I arrive everywhere, except airports, where it's three hours before departure. Back to prison.

Legal visits are between 2 and 4pm. In this particular penitentiary it takes between 15 and 30 minutes to go through various stages of security checking. First, there is a solemnly celebrated task to find the prisoner on the list, then comes fingerprint identification for regular offenders, I mean visitors, visitors. The fingerprint scanner can be temperamental, which can cause security guards to work themselves up into a state, which in turn delays the ceremony further.

Today, however, I do not even get to experience the doubtful pleasures of rolling my finger up and down the scanner. The solicitors have not turned up.

Priorities

Today I am dealing with a guy who had been playing hide-and-seek with law enforcement for the last three years. It caught up with him yesterday after somebody informed the police about his whereabouts.

He had previously been given bail in extradition proceedings. Not wishing to be sent back to Poland, a few months later he cut off his electronic tag and went underground. Because he absconded from one set of court proceedings, he then decided, for consistency's sake not to comply with a court order issued in another matter and failed to fulfil the requirement to report to the police annually in relation to a sexual assault conviction. He had been put on sexual offenders register for 7 years some time before the extradition case came to light.

Today he is going to get a short prison sentence in relation to the domestic matter and his extradition case will resume on completion of this sentence. He is wanted in Poland to serve 3 years for robbery and a string of minor other offences.

His current circumstances could be described with high degree of accuracy as a bit of a pickle.

And yet, the only question he had for his solicitor and me this morning was last night's Poland football game result.

The moment I told him Poland lost to Senegal, including an own goal, he broke down completely.

Funny thing, priorities.

Waiting Room

Cold damp morning at Magistrates Court, 9.15, small waiting room packed full of people who would rather be elsewhere, myself included. Tired indifferent faces. Ushers read out names. Boredom sets in quickly.

- 'Baby shark do do do do do'

- 'When I was in prison, George Michael came in...'

- 'Mr X, we have reviewed the tape and you might get a surprise when you see....'

- Mummy shark do do do do do'

- 'And they said to us go to your cells, there is nothing to see'

- 'Daddy shark...'

Greek

- 'Mr Y and madam interpreter please come into the courtroom and sit at the back'

We go in, the previous case has not finished.

- 'Mr N, do you plead guilty not guilty or no indication of plea to the charge of sexual grooming of a person under 16?'

- 'Guilty'

- 'Very well, your case will be referred to crown court for sentencing'

My client wants to know what's going on. I summarise that the guy in the dock just pleaded guilty to sexual grooming of a 13-year-old or, more specifically felt into an online trap set up by the police.

- A paedophile! My client exclaims in disgust.

The word sounds almost identical in Polish, we all learnt Greek from the same sources.

All eyes on me.

Christmas

You know it's Christmas when a defence lawyer at court says this in mitigation:

'Your honour, he is clearly not a very good thief. He attempted bulk theft of baby milk formula for the second time in less than a month, and he got caught both times. He stated in his interview that the milk was for his baby. He now tells me that his son is 3 years old and clearly does not need Aptamil anymore. He cannot even maintain a consistent lie from one day to the next. He would like to be treated leniently today so he can still go back to Poland for Christmas. Unless I can assist any further'.

Box of Chocolates

Life as a court interpreter really is like a box of chocolates. I never know what I will get until I meet my client on the day. Magistrates' court job can mean anything from a speeding ticket, theft from Tesco's, domestic assault, up to administrative first appearance in rape, or murder case only for the matter to be transferred to the crown court to be processed further.

Today I deal with two mothers summoned to court for not sending their children to school as often as is customary in this country. Both happen to have children at the same school. As we wait, they begin to talk. As we wait longer, they begin to forge a plan for today's hearings. Their children managed 82% and 70% attendance during last school year. The 70% mother says to the 82% one, I don't think it is our fault, it must be the school. My daughter has bouts of diarrhoea and vomiting when she comes home, it must be the school lunches that make her sick. I am going to plead not guilty. She tries to bend the 82% to her way of thinking, but she fails. That puts her in a bad mood. I become her next target, have you got children, do they have good attendance, are you happy with school dinners? She gets three Yes's from me, which makes her even grumpier. I know better than to tell her that my daughters had 100% attendance for the last couple of years, and if they have a mild cold they still go to school. She might request a different interpreter quoting conflict of interest.

Snow

First time for everything. Today's case was abandoned due to adverse weather conditions, specifically a few snow flurries which had flickered across Kent.

The judge was there, as was the defence barrister, the prosecutor, the interpreter, the officer in the case, the court clerk and the usher. The defendant wasn't there.

The prison van did not make it to court today. We went to the listing office to re-book the hearing.

- When would you like it re-booked for?

We unleashed all the bottled-up wit and verbal virtuosity we were saving up for use in the courtroom.

- When it hasn't snowed for a few days.

- When the snow has melted.

- A few weeks after clocks go forward

- Mid-July?

Wrong Job?

As I join a small army of smartly suited solicitors, probation officers, clerks, ushers and interpreters in our purposeful stride from East Croydon station, Costa and Nero cups our meagre weapons against Monday morning misery, I watch several lots of designer-clad, heavily tattooed defendants (innocent until proven guilty) and their entourages pouring out of black cabs just outside court door, Ray-bans glistening, Michael Kors handbags swinging.

What am I doing wrong?

Humor

Just when I thought my clients were losing their sense of humour.

- If found guilty today, you will be disqualified from driving for the period of 12 to 18 months, is this going to cause you a problem?

- It will definitely make my life more difficult, your honour, but it will not be a huge problem, as I don't even have a licence.

My Craft

In this final chapter, I would like to give you a glimpse of what is involved in my craft, and what linguistic challenges I am up against on a daily basis.

I know I am a good interpreter. So much so that some of my English-speaking clients seem to believe I am in fact a machine. One of them said to me today, 'please transfer this data and then stand by for more input.' I chose to take it as a compliment.

Whenever I am booked to interpret for a defendant in a crown court trial, once we establish that the trial is actually effective and is actually going to go ahead and run its course, rather than be adjourned, or abandoned, I start preparing myself, mentally and linguistically, for the highlight of my role, which will come when the defendant is giving evidence.

Language related hurdles of court interpreting are manifold.

Specialist terminology is being thrown at us with the assumption that we are natural born bilingual experts in cannabis cultivation equipment, replica firearms types, vehicle adaptation for purposes of people smuggling, and whichever other crime our clients try their luck in.

Interpreters are not briefed in advance about the nature of allegations our clients are facing, so there is no time to do any background research on 'context'.

Defendant's vocabulary is often limited, and their grammar is, well, their own. They often answer in disjointed broken sentences, they stop and start, and occasionally throw in something entirely for my, the interpreter's benefit, which makes my job and the chance of the listeners' following what I am saying on his behalf challenging.

I am obliged to 'interpreter everything that is being said'. This mantra is repeated ad nauseam in all interpreting guidelines and codes of practice, and accuracy of rendition is a major criteria in all industry exams. Aiming to interpret everything that is being said is an admirable ideal to strive towards, but real-life scenarios are rarely ideal.

- What did you do next Mr X, after going into the corner shop to buy cigarettes?

- Oh my god, what is his problem, twenty questions on what I did on the way to work, step by step, it's a farce, a comedy, ok, fine, please do not interpret this, tell him I just got to work, alright, tell him I can't remember what I did every second along that journey, what an idiot!

My clients do not attend interpreting courses so the idea that they are not supposed to engage into a side conversation with the interpreter is not properly ingrained in their minds. I always mention this rule to them before going to the witness box, but nerves and stress often get the better of them once the prosecutor starts firing questions at them, and rules of working with an interpreter escape them, so I am left to deal with the aftermath of their undisciplined linguistic behaviour.

In the above scenario, I have two choices. First, I interpret everything that the defendant just said to me, including 'tell him I just got to work' which might not be immediately understandable to my audience, and often prompts a confused 'sorry, what do you mean Mr X, tell who you just got to work?' or, I raise my hand, and begin by, 'this is the interpreter speaking, the defendant has just addressed me directly with a comment, and then asked me not to interpret it, may I remind the defendant that I am obliged to interpret everything he says and to direct his answer directly to the person who is asking the question?'.

On occasion, clients challenge my linguistic agility and my ability to think fast to its limits.

- When she asked you why you did not turn up at the flat as agreed, what did you say to her?

- The defendant looked at me, opened his mouth, closed it, opened again, and said this, in his native Polish, with clear irritation in his voice.

- Co? Jajco!

He then went back to methodically picking dirt from behind his thumbnail, a cue for me that he finished replying to the question and I should feel free to begin interpreting.

His two-word answer rhymes in Polish, and is very short. The jury might have picked up on the rhyming bit, the two words are pronounced, Tsoh? Yaytsoh. The brevity of the answer would not have escaped them either. I am thinking, I am thinking, and, a couple of seconds later, a stroke of genius on my part no less, I say:

- What? Squat!

Which was as good a translation of his answer warranted.

The other side gives me headaches too. Barristers' questions are often grammatically and stylistically convoluted, punctuated by abundant use of legal doublets, a scattering of French and Latin, with an occasional sudden switch to the defendant's vernacular for added oratory effect.

'*Did you deem this a suitable attire to don on the occasion of ....*' the advocate intones, tugging at the lapels of his Harry Potteresque black gown.

I remind myself that I am here to facilitate successful communication between two linguistically incompatible parties, so I make sure I translate this as 'did you think these were suitable clothes to wear to...', otherwise we are facing a few rounds of, sorry, could you repeat that, I don't understand the question, what do you mean, I am not sure what you are asking me, and so on.

Occasionally, lawyers doubt my level of fluency in English, and choose to question it in unexpected moments. One lawyer did not bat an eye lid when throwing words and phrases like *pulchritude, a fortiori, and ad idem* during their questioning, but then he suddenly addressed me directly and asked, interpreter do you know what I mean when I use the term *hit a nail on its head?* Yes, I do. Oh, good, good, I am trying to keep my language simple for the benefit of everybody here. No, you are not. I say the last bit in my head only.

Sarcasm can be tricky, even without an interpreter in the middle.

My clients are prone to losing their temper when challenged, and resort to aggressive sarcasm on a regular basis.

- Yes sir, I did bash his head in. You should look him over for other injuries too, because I probably caused them too, and if I'd had more time, I would've killed his cat too, but I was running late for work.

How do I know the complainant? Gee, let me think, I have no idea, possibly because I am married to his sister, do you think this can be it?

The above flights of defendants' wit need to be rendered in a similarly sarcastic tone of voice, mocking facial expression might help too, but of course I have to be apply the sarcasm and them mockery sparingly, so it is clear that they come from the client, and not directly from me, the interpreter. A minefield.

Perpetrators of low level, alcohol and poverty fuelled crime often experience only the briefest encounter with education, which affects their ability to communicate with others in later life. Add to it an acute deficit of social skills and a permanent undercurrent of anger, and the result is very poor quality of verbal expression. Enter the interpreter, who is supposed to convey accurately what the defendant is saying in their own language. So far so good, but when I start giving ungrammatical, incomprehensible answers to legal professionals' questions in court, it is often me, not the defendant, who is getting funny looks from the audience, as they think it is me who is unable to speak in full sentences, and that I only have a tentative grip on English grammar.

It is not uncommon for the defendant to answer the simple question, where do you work? with, *I mean, well, I did but, I mean, you know, last week, recently I have, do I have to, right now, at the moment, so no, not this week.* After my best attempt to interpret the above accurately, it is not uncommon for jury members to wonder whether I am best suited for the role.

I like to think that I take it all in my stride rather well, and as practice makes perfect, I must be getting better at negotiating communication between the two parties that rely on me heavily on each occasion. I never know what challenge awaits behind each new courtroom door and this is possibly the single biggest reason why I can see myself opening new doors for quite some time yet.

Q&A – Do Judges Have Hammers?

The Q&A section was initially inspired by my husband, who has been asking me a lot of searching questions about inner workings of British courts over the years, he still does. I then took the Q&A project further and asked all my friends to ask me questions, any questions, about any aspect of court proceedings which was unclear to them, to make this section thoroughly comprehensive. Insert chapter nine text here.

Do judges have hammers?

No. In the UK, hammers are reserved for auctioneers to seal the sale.

And it is called a gavel, not a hammer. Judges in Britain never used gavels, but it is an easy mistake to make, we have all watched too many US courtroom dramas, where judges use gavels a lot.

Why do they wear wigs?

Like so many other things, it is steeped in tradition. At some point, the 18th century is the usual culprit for this sort of things, it became fashionable for men of elevated social status to wear them. Why do they still wear them in the 21st century, when every other part of society dispensed with them? I researched that part of the question thoroughly, and the best answer I could find is this, courtesy of the Modern Notion website; 'they continue to wear them because nobody has ever told them to stop'.

How do you become a judge/magistrate?

To become a judge in a crown court or higher, you need to study law, then after you graduate you need to continue to study law at postgraduate level, at some point taking a bar exam, after which you become a barrister, and you are on your route to judgedom. At any given crown court trial, you will be forgiven for thinking that judges tend to side with the prosecution. Officially, judges are fully impartial referees who oversee proceedings to make sure that the law of the land is applied correctly, but defendants and defence barristers often have their own opinions about that. Come to court and see for yourself, most trials are open to the public to watch, and if you cannot afford a TV licence, you might consider watching a live trial as a temporary measure.

To become a magistrate, you need to be a decent member of society and complete an application form which you can download from the gov.uk website.

How does a Magistrates Court compare to a Crown Court and to the Old Bailey?

Magistrates' Court is a lower court, where all criminal cases begin their life. Everybody who has been charged with an offence is initially brought to a Magistrates' Court for their first appearance. In case of serious charges, such as murder, manslaughter, GBH, the first appearance is very brief and all that happens is that the case is committed to the Crown Court for the remainder of the proceedings.

This has to do with sentencing powers of Magistrates' Courts which are not sufficient in case of serious crime, as the maximum custodial sentence they can impose is usually six months imprisonment, and in some scenarios up to 12 months imprisonment.

Do prisoners wear handcuffs?

As soon as a prisoner is produced at court they are referred to as a defendant for the day. As a general rule, defendants do not wear handcuffs in the courtroom, unless exceptional circumstances apply. The idea is not to prejudice the jury against the defendant. I have never had a defendant handcuffed in the dock, not even in a murder trial. A fancy term for the defendant being un-handcuffed is that he is unfettered.

Do they wear prison uniforms?

It's complicated. One thing for sure, they do not wear orange overalls. A typical prison uniform in the UK consists of a track suit in a dull shade of grey, which some, but not all prisoners wear at court.

Remand prisoners, i.e. those whose bail has been refused and they await the outcome of their case in prison, are allowed to wear their own clothes. Prisoners are also allowed to wear their own clothes during their trial.

Can you escape from court?

Depends on your role in the proceedings. Judges and barristers escape effortlessly, they aim to leave the building by 5pm at the latest, and they are usually successful.

For a defendant in the dock, escape would be tricky. The dock usually has glass panel going all the way to the ceiling, with narrow slits to allow papers to be passed to the defendant. There are courts where the glass does not go all the way up, but looks like a windshield in a convertible with the roof down, other courts have open wooden docks, and that does present a potential opportunity for a defendant to jump over the dock barrier, run out of the courtroom, and barge through the front door, successfully mowing down security guards as they go. I have not experienced such an attempt at first hand, so I cannot discuss the feasibility of it.

Do you swear on the Bible, and why? What happens if you are an atheist, Muslim, Hindu?

Before giving evidence in court each witness is sworn in. The usher will ask them routinely, 'do you wish to swear on a holy book or affirm?' but even that simple question might be confusing if you are a first-timer. Witnesses are spoilt for choice when it comes to which book, they wish to consider holy. New Testament, Old Testament, Koran, and a couple other books which I never see because they are always kept in green or yellow velvet pouches, and only taken out when needed, but they are available, so Hindu and Sikh witnesses can swear on their own holy books.

As to the why part of the question, tradition strikes again, a person was firmly believed to be more likely to tell the truth if they swore by Almighty God to do so.

Atheists say the words of an affirmation rather than the oath, which reads ' I do solemnly, sincerely and truly declare and affirm that the evidence I shall give shall be the truth, the whole truth and nothing but the truth'.

Glossary

The glossary has been compiled as an attempt to explain all the intriguing legal terms used in the book in a main in the street friendly manner. It does not replace Wikipedia, but it offers an alternative.

American English

The language which adds further complication to already confusing legal terminology in Britain.

In recent years Legally Blonde films have a lot to answer for. Attorney, felony, larceny, grand jury, writ, and even testimony are just a few examples of terms you are not likely to hear in British courts.

Basis of Plea

Partial admission of guilt. Usually expressed as, 'I am guilty, but…' In case of an assault the defendant might wish to plead guilty to some facts alleged by the Prosecution whilst denying others, so for example he might say, yeah, I slapped her in the face with an open hand twice, but I did not drag her on the floor by her hair and did not kick her in the stomach.

Bench

A collective noun for magistrates. Like a romp of otters or a prickle of porcupines. 'The bench will retire now' translates that the magistrates will collectively get up, and walk out of the courtroom for a while, possibly to make a decision about an issue on the case they are handling.

Either way offence

An offence that can be tried either by the Magistrates' Court or the Crown Court. In these cases, the defendant has the right to choose whether they want to be tried in a lower court by the Magistrates' or in the Crown Court by the jury.

Hostile witness

A prosecution witness who refuses to give evidence to support the prosecution case. This happens quite a lot in cases originating in domestic settings, where one of the partners, typically a woman, willingly gives a statement testifying against her previous partner in the initial stages of police investigation, but by the time his trial takes place, often months later, she changes her mind and does not wish to give evidence against him in court. She dodges the prosecution questions, and says that she cannot remember or is no longer sure about anything relating to the events in question. This potentially puts prosecution and their case in a spot of bother, especially in classic 'his word against hers' scenarios.

Magistrate

A magistrate is a lay person, a volunteer, and at least initially, an amateur in the legal profession, some of the magistrates become impressively well versed in good old legal rules and lingo at the end of their stint on the bench. The only qualification a magistrate needs is to be a decent member of society, upstanding is the word some people like to use to describe them. Magistrates sit at Magistrates Courts across the land, there is never just one magistrate, and they form a panel of two or three. As magistrates are not qualified lawyers, there is always a legal adviser that sits in a row in front of them and makes sure that law is applied properly to each case that magistrates preside over.

Newton hearing

Whenever I do not wish to overburden a client who is facing a Newton hearing with too much complex information, I just say that it is a mini-trial, and their barrister is usually happy with this, as it keeps matters simple. Based on my experience, a Newton hearing takes place when a defendant pleads guilty but is willing to admit a significantly different set of facts than the one that the Prosecution alleges against them. Newton hearing takes place in front of judge only, without the jury. On such occasions the judge puts a proper judge's hat on top of his wig, well, obviously not literally, he doesn't, and decides who is more likely to be telling the truth. The name comes from the name of a defendant in a 1983 case R v Newton. Newton hearing is also called a trial of issue.

R v Smith

R stands for Regina, which stands for the Queen, it can also stand for Rex, which stands for the King, which is convenient I suppose. V is an abbreviation of Latin term versus, which means against. Smith is a sample name of the defendant against whom Regina, i.e. the Queen, but really the CPS i.e. the Crown Prosecution Service decided to instigate court proceedings.

Printed in Great Britain
by Amazon